ENGAGE AND PASSION AND PURPOSE WITH PEOPLE EMPOWER AND

The RELATIONSHIP CODE

MARGARET McCRAW
PhD, MBA

CAREER
PRESS

D1113817

THE RELATIONSHIP CODE
EDITED AND TYPESET BY KARA KUMPEL
Cover design by Howard Grossman/ 12E Designs
Printed in the U.S.A. by Courier

To order this title, please call toll-free 1-800-CAREER-1 (NJ and Canada: 201-848-0310) to order using VISA or MasterCard, or for further information on books from Career Press.

CAREER
PRESS

The Career Press, Inc.
220 West Parkway, Unit 12
Pompton Plains, NJ 07444
www.careerpress.com

Library of Congress Cataloging-in-Publication Data
McCraw, Margaret.
   The relationship code: engage and empower people with purpose and passion / by Margaret McCraw.
      p. cm.
   Includes bibliographical references and index.
   ISBN 978-1-60163-135-0 -- ISBN 978-1-60163-708-6 (ebook) 1. Interpersonal relations--Psychological aspects. 2. Interpersonal communication. I. Title.

HM1106.M39 2010
158.2--dc22

                                                            2010025468

This book is dedicated to my birth family. Thank you for walking the path of life with me, and for your abundance of love, white light, and many lessons learned.

My mother, Ethel Sumner McCraw, helped me to see that my peace of mind and sense of well-being do not depend on anything outside of me. She consistently modeled emotional strength, will, perseverance, and determination.

My father, Arthur McCraw, gave me the opportunity to learn the deeper lessons of forgiveness and compassion. I am more whole because of what I learned from my relationship with him.

My sister, Shirley McCraw-Garlan, showed me that true love transcends time and space. Thank you for uplifting me on many occasions and for always being there for me.

My brother, Ken McCraw, led me to realize the strength of my spirit. He's always been someone I could count on.

My sister, Mary McCraw-Borst, is my friend and partner as we have learned to release and transcend deep emotional pain. Thank you for being there for me.

My brother, David McCraw, helped me to know that I am a good friend. Since childhood, he has inspired me to greater heights.

ACKNOWLEDGMENTS

I am appreciative of the many individuals who helped me to bring this book forth. First, my agent, JoAnn Deck, who believed in my work and who made a strong commitment to help me bring this material into the public's view. In addition, her review and input to the book itself was invaluable. There were many late nights, but we did it!

I also want to extend warm appreciation to Michael Aschenbach, the whistling swan, who provided the consistent support and skill set to bring my work to light. You are a dear soul.

Thank you, Karen Greathouse, for your support during the proposal stage of this book. Your input and assistance is much appreciated.

I want to extend heartfelt appreciation to Barbara Ardinger, PhD, the best editor anyone could ever ask for. I especially appreciate you working into the night and on weekends to ensure that I met my deadline with the publisher.

My appreciation is also extended to Sue Gaines, the graphic artist who worked on short notice to bring my diagrams to life, and to Joanne Sprott, who was also willing to work quickly to assist me in finalizing the book. I am deeply grateful to Julia Mastin and Jasmine Mastin who worked long hours to proofread the final manuscript. Thank you for all you did to make the final product even better.

Many dear friends and family members offered love and support along the way; you know who you are—thank you! J.R. Oyler stands out in the crowd for his consistent support, encouragement, and help in getting the manuscript to the publisher on time. Tom Kapp provided ongoing love, encouragement, and appreciation for my work.

I extend gratitude to the staff of Career Press for their commitment to offering books that are uplifting to individuals. Thank you all for believing in my work and for your efforts in bringing this book to fruition.

I am deeply grateful to Esther and Jerry Hicks and the family of Abraham. Your teachings on vibrational alignment and being a deliberate creator have been life-changing. Thank you for raising the consciousness of myself and others. You are a great gift to the Universe.

I also give thanks to the great teachers who have strongly influenced me: Dr. Carl Gustav Jung, Saint Barnabus, and the light of Saint Paul. Thank you for the timeless teachings and guidance you brought to the world.

Finally, I acknowledge those loved ones who reside in my heart and my mind forever: Sr. Suzanne Marie Folie; Dr. Art Wagner; my mother, Ethel Sumner McCraw; my grandmother, Mary Ann Gennettie Ellen Sumner; and Nathaniel, Phillip, Precious, Benny, Star, Shadow, and many other family members and friends. Thank you for supporting me and inspiring me to greater heights.

I love all of you so much.

CONTENTS

Author's Note   9

Foreword by Brian Billick   11

Preface: Treasure What You Have   15

Introduction   21

Harmonic Matching (A poem by the author)   25

Part I—Insights Into Your Relationships

Chapter 1: What Is the Harmonic
Matching Process?   29

Chapter 2: Self-Understanding:
The Foundation of Successful
Relationships   47

Chapter 3: Co-Create With Others   69

Chapter 4: How to Recover From
the Loss of a Relationship   89

Part II—Harmonic Matching: Four Steps to Fulfill Relationship Intentions

Chapter 5: Step One: Create
Feel-Good Moments   119

Chapter 6: Step Two: Identify Your Desires   145

Chapter 7: Step Three: Activate
Your Intentions   163

Chapter 8: Step Four: Release the Outcome   185

Conclusion   215

Appendix: Frequently Asked Questions   221

Glossary   235

Bibliography   243

What Will You Do? (A poem by the author)   247

Index   249

About the Author   253

Author's Note

Case examples presented in this book are composites of different situations to protect individuals' identities. Similarities between these anecdotes and the experiences of actual persons are unintended.

Life coaches specializing in the four-step Harmonic Matching Process are referenced in a few chapters in this book; an accredited fast-track life coach training program has been established to certify individuals as a Master Life Coach and Holistic Health Practitioner. See the back of this book for training and certification information.

The phrase *highest good* is used throughout this book. It is not intended to convey a religious connotation. You, the reader, are welcome to substitute the term *best interest* if you are more comfortable with that.

T*he Relationship Code* is for individuals and organizational leaders who have a vision they intend to achieve. Leadership requires building strong, resilient teams with people who are knowledgeable and mutually supportive. It is about creating relationships, which means understanding the psychology of what holds people together and what tears them apart. Basic tenets, such as being open-minded, getting out of your own way, aligning with the highest good of all, and blending heart wisdom with sound logic are just a few of the building blocks necessary to create a bond with others. You must have integrity at the highest levels. Above all, you must believe in yourself, for this is the foundation on which all relationships are built. Without self-belief, there can be no trust, no respect, and no true bond with another person. When you are clear in your values and have the courage to stand up for your beliefs, you have something meaningful to give to another person. You can truly create with others. You can be a team.

I have spent much of my life building winning teams, and guided the Baltimore Ravens to become Super Bowl champions. Team-building is about creating strong and synergistic relationships with individuals who respect and trust their leader as well as each other. Relationships require emotional strength, self-examination, self-reflection, and a willingness to make changes. These are all necessary components of a true connection. Harmonizing desires with others requires letting go of "me" in favor of "we," yet always being true to yourself. Forming a bond means taking a risk, because at some point and in some way life brings circumstances that will change what you have created, which requires you to trust and let go and experience what feels like loss. Fear of loss is the reason people resist change. This is why we hold ourselves back, and it is also why organizations are prevented from achieving their vision. Leaders need to deal with loss in order to break new ground and transform the organization.

In *The Relationship Code*, Dr. Margaret McCraw provides a dynamic guide filled with practical tools leaders can use to create successful teams—on the field, in the workplace, or at home—that enhance the strength of the organization as well as the family unit. Dr. McCraw coaches readers in creating a strong and resilient workforce aligned with passion and purpose. Her guidance provides a clear, unique four-step model, the Harmonic Matching Process, which can be used to create relationship goals and desires of all kinds, thus bringing synergy to the workplace. Individuals are better able to work together for the higher good of the organization. Dr. McCraw's 25 years as a licensed psychotherapist and seasoned organizational consultant have taught her to blend behavioral principles with business logic and ageless wisdom. She draws on her entire life experience to address an extremely important and relevant topic that impacts each of us at home and at work.

The development of the subject matter in this book is superb. It moves you from understanding vibrational consciousness to applying this insight to your relationships. You learn to bridge differences, be true to yourself, communicate better, harmonize your desires, align with others, build a team, and activate your intentions.

In my work as a motivational speaker and consultant, I have identified 12 principles of success. I wrote about these in *Competitive Leadership*. These principles were the foundation for guiding the Ravens to win the Super Bowl. I have used them over and over again in my work with organizations to help them create winning teams. Dr. McCraw's four-step Harmonic Matching Process integrates these principles into a sound method that aligns energy and creates relationship goals. The Harmonic Matching Process teaches you how to be a winner at life, both personally and professionally.

The tools in this book will help you in all aspects of your life. You will be able to create powerful and enjoyable relationships, while meeting other life goals and dreams. As you move through Dr. McCraw's four-step model and begin to correlate your thoughts, beliefs, and emotions with what you are attracting, you will become very skilled in manifesting things you have always wanted.

Allow Dr. McCraw to be your personal guide. Follow her lead and create purpose and passion—prerequisites for allowing happiness and abundance to flow in your life and your organization. In my opinion, her lifelong mission to inspire purposeful, passionate, and joyous living has been achieved in this book. Her unique marriage of psychological knowledge and business principles, coupled with the tremendous success of her clients, is a testament to the effectiveness of her Harmonic Matching Process.

Winning at life begins in your mind. You must cultivate a winning consciousness. When your purpose is clear, your passion is strong, and you align your beliefs with your desires, your ability to create is limitless. Trust in your own well-being and know that your life dreams are before you, ready to unfold into miraculous achievements.

Brian Billick
Super Bowl–Winning Coach,
Author of *Competitive Leadership: 12 Principles for Success*
July 2010

PREFACE:
Treasure What You Have

This book comes to you from my heart and my soul. I bring it to you in hopes that it will support you in creating a lifetime of joy. Much of the knowledge imparted in these pages has grown from the relationships I've had with the ones I loved the most, beginning with my relationship with my mother. It has been said that our families are our greatest teachers; I believe this to be true. When I was young, there were many misunderstandings between my mother and me, and the words we spoke often caused unnecessary pain; our unspoken messages broke our hearts. Both of us had built walls of defense mechanisms around ourselves that prevented us from resolving the issues we struggled with for many years. None of this would have been so painful had we been more compassionate with each other. I am grateful that through the years I learned this fact and was finally able to find peace, joy, and resolution in my relationship with my mother.

What I did not understand during my younger years is that love knows no pain and that the heart holds no fear. Pain and fear are things we unknowingly invite into our consciousness when we judge ourselves or others, when we try to change someone into the person we want him or her to be for our own edification. Pain will always be present until we replace judgment of ourselves and others with compassion. When we stop judging, we close the door to the things that hold us back in life. When we understand that compassion is the language of the heart and the key to all good relationships, that's when blame ceases to exist. When we stop trying to control others— whether they are our children, our spouses, or our parents— that's when we free ourselves to enjoy this journey called life. We learn our lessons about interacting with each other as we stumble along the way.

Each of us has choices to make. When we fall on the path of life, we can choose to harden our heart and to find peace and solace in residing in our head. We can build a fortress that no man or woman can enter. Or we can look at ourselves with compassion and decide to gain clarity and understanding every time we fall. Learning from our missteps will bring us to the higher ground, where we can get a fuller view of the circumstances, detach or release our errors with love, and move forward to a deeper level of relationship with ourselves and with others.

The Relationship Code is a guide for readers in their personal and professional relationships. That is, it can be used both at home and in the workplace. My goal in writing this book has been to reach people who can benefit from my many years of experience as a licensed therapist, executive coach, and management consultant. I believe that wherever we work, our place of work is a rich playground where we can learn from each other, and apply this knowledge in our families too. It is important to bring our lessons home, where the stakes are much higher. We can get a new job, new coworkers, and new colleagues, and re-create our work life in a new organization, but we cannot so easily replace our parents, our children, our siblings, or other important people in our lives. The stakes really are the highest at home because families so often hold on to pain and misunderstandings from years gone by, oftentimes not even telling each other what they are really upset about, or perhaps not even remembering what caused the misunderstanding to begin with.

Like yours, my own life has been filled with bumps along the road. As a young woman, I unknowingly placed my peace of mind and happiness on hold, waiting for family members to align with well-being and happiness. I unconsciously absorbed their pain. In time, thank goodness, I learned that you cannot help another person by taking on their pain, by sacrificing your life for theirs, or even just by offering sympathy. Absorbing someone else's pain immobilizes you. It sends the other person a nonverbal message that you do not trust in their well-being, that you do not believe in their ability to overcome obstacles. We're taught that giving is better than receiving, but this sacrificial "giving" involves *giving up* rather than *giving*. It says to the other person that you do not believe he can do something on his own. That's why you, the "stronger" of the two, are taking control and "helping" them. But this is not a gift from the heart. In order to offer something of value to another, we often have to replace sacrifice and sorrow with holding the vision of his strength. Offer empathy and compassion to others; don't try to take control of them. Be a thoughtful and loving friend because you want to be, not from obligation, guilt, or fear of regret.

Relationships are matters of the heart, but they are integrated with the logic of your mind and your conscience. When I review my past experiences, any situation I now wish I'd handled differently involved making a decision in which I left out my heart. When we leave out our hearts, we step out of integrity, and it is lack of integrity that causes people to have regrets. This book is about living from the highest degree of integrity. It's about taking any undesirable experience or regret we have and turning it into a learning experience. By learning from challenging (and often unpleasant) circumstances, we create new desires that keep us moving in a positive direction. We no longer remain stuck in our past unpleasantnesses. If we don't learn from our experiences, then we keep repeating the same mistakes until we finally learn what we need to learn. Over and over, I see marriages end in divorce, and then I see each person connect with a new partner and the same unresolved issues arise in the new relationship. Over and over, I see individuals leaving jobs and moving to new ones where they attract the same issues with their new employer, boss, or direct reports.

As a young senior manager, I also experienced various ups and downs in my workplace, continuing to attract the same undesirable circumstances until I made a decision to look deeper in the mirror. As I became more aware of how my management style impacted others, for better or for worse, I made changes in myself. I learned to lead from a place of integrity and wholeness and to bring about a positive transformation in my workplace. My changes in myself impacted the people around me in both my personal and professional lives.

Later, as I moved into my own business as an organizational consultant, I made a commitment to help my clients achieve their dreams. As an entrepreneur, I created my own vision and learned more about integrating sound psychological principles with organizational dynamics. I also discovered what worked and what did not work on a practical level. This is how the four-step Harmonic Matching Process was developed. I worked with and applied the four steps to my own work for many years until I perfected the steps and the principles that my clients also found to be highly effective. The Harmonic Matching Process provides you with the tools you need to create dynamic relationships and successful outcomes for yourself at home and at work.

This book about relationships is filled with techniques that have worked not only for me but also for my clients, both individuals and organizations, for many years. These tools will help you too. You will gain valuable knowledge to enhance all of your relationships, make deeper and more satisfying connections with friends, family, colleagues, and coworkers, and align with purpose and passion. This is the foundation for experiencing joy. By sharing my experiences from my life and from people with whom I've worked, I have fulfilled the intentions of my heart and soul: to inspire purpose, and passionate, joyous living. It is my hope that readers who can benefit from the information I have imparted will attract this book to uplift them and give them the knowledge I so longed for during my years of upheaval with the ones I loved the most.

It is with a deep sense of purpose and passion that I hold you in my heart as you read the pages that unfold.

Margaret McCraw, PhD, MBA, LCSW-C
Baltimore, Maryland
July 2010

INTRODUCTION

People with positive social relationships recover from illness faster.
—Robert Wood Johnson Foundation

Strong & Sustained Intimacy Helps You Live Longer.
—American Psychological Association

Family is the most pressing concern of 22 percent of all women.
—Gallup News Service

*People who have a "best friend" at work are seven
times more likely to be engaged in their jobs.*
—Gallup Management Journal

*Conflicted Feelings About a Relationship
Can Raise Your Blood Pressure.*
—Marriage and Families study

*Fifty-four percent of Americans fight with people close
to them because of stress.*
—American Psychological Association

Many of us are greatly affected by our daily interactions with those whom we regularly encounter, whether these people are our bosses, coworkers, families, or friends. These relationships can be major contributors to our overall success at work and at home, our health, and our well-being.

Our reaction to challenging situations and conflict in our relationships causes stress, which is a psychological and physiological response to events that upset our personal balance in some way. We have all experienced relationships that have caused tension, and anxiety within us. Although the stressors in our daily lives play a major role in our overall health, happiness, and productivity, many of us believe that we have no control over these.

It is important to respond to challenges and conflict in a manner that prevents or at least minimizes stress that affects our health. It is crucial, therefore, that we explore the dynamics of our interpersonal relationships and understand how we attract negative or positive experiences. Our current state of well-being is mirrored through our thoughts, beliefs, and emotions, creating experiences that shape our daily lives. We must learn how to create positive vibrations and shape our own destinies.

We must first understand how our thoughts and emotions affect our mental and physical well-being. The World Health Organization states, in its Constitution, "Mental health is not just the absence of mental disorder. It is defined as a state of well-being in which *every individual realizes his or her own potential, can cope with the normal stresses of life, can work productively and fruitfully, and is able to make a contribution to her or his community.*"

To recognize our own potential, we must believe in ourselves and understand our potential to contribute to the higher good for all. We must take responsibility for our lives without judgment, guilt, or blame, because these factors can lower our belief in our self-worth and turn us into some of the alarming statistics quoted here. Let us let go of those painful memories from our past once and for all. By releasing judgment and negative thoughts, we create positive energy and attract more of what we desire. Let us take responsibility for our feelings and realize that no one can make us feel good or bad. Let us be true to ourselves and understand that we can only love others as much as we love ourselves.

We must learn to cope with the challenges of life in a positive manner. Think about your colleagues, family, and friends; do you ever encounter tension in any of these relationships? How we deal with them is the difference between a healthy mental state and an unhealthy one. To begin eliminating interpersonal stress, we must understand what causes tension in these relationships and begin effectively communicating with others. Learning to respond rather than merely react is a common challenge. To reach our highest potential, we must communicate with others openly, honestly, thoughtfully, respectfully, and genuinely. Authentic communication will lead us to greater interpersonal relationships that will benefit all. We will be heard and respected as we interact with others.

The Harmonic Matching Process explained in this book will help you in all aspects of your life. You will be able to create positive relationships with colleagues, bosses, friends, spouses, and family members. You can even apply this system to enhance your emotional and physical health, financial and career success, along with other desires. As you work with the four-step Harmonic Matching Process, you will become very powerful in creating a consciousness aligned with all of your desires. You are limitless in your ability to create fulfillment when the passion is high, the intent is pure, and the "knowing" is strong. The concepts are simple, but the application is complex, which explains why so many people never make the leap from feeling trapped in their jobs, frustrated at home, and victimized by others, to taking charge of their lives.

This book will look at various kinds of interpersonal relationships and examine how our beliefs, thoughts, and feelings attract both positive and negative situations to us. It will teach you how to effectively communicate with your family, colleagues, boss, and friends, and, moreover, to be heard, understood, and respected by them. It will also guide you to deeper levels of understanding and give you specifics on how to shift your negative experiences into positive opportunities that allow you to receive more of what you are truly seeking and less of what you find undesirable.

Enjoy this fascinating and exhilarating guide to your relationships. It will enhance your health and well-being. It will guide you to greater truths and insights that will empower you to live your destiny. Open your mind and heart and begin the journey of discovery as you learn how to shift your consciousness and optimize your own energies into a powerful magnetic force. You have already taken the first step; now continue forward on this path of discovery, for it holds with it all that you desire.

Harmonic Matching

Consciousness does exist
throughout the Universe, in the mist,
to help you create your relationship bliss.

What if one day you made a new choice,
enabling your heart to open and rejoice?

Releasing old pain—letting go of your tears,
with the ones in your life you held so dear,
including those at work you previously feared.
Allowing your life to be open and clear.

Choose to stop placing your well-being on hold
by commanding your subconscious to take control,
allowing your relationship dreams to unfold.

Create feel-good moments right from the start,
you move to step two, by doing your part.
Making your wish list you feel very smart.
You know what you want—it's straight from your
heart.

Step three is important, it requires some thought,
to prevent your psyche from becoming distraught.
It's the staircase that strengthens your belief in this
matter,
goals and objectives that create the ladder.

Activating intentions you stay strong and wise,
mind over matter to enable the prize.

On to step four so you can open the door,
this looks familiar, you've been here before.
Enabling compassion to penetrate your heart,
forgoing the burdens that kept you apart.

Co-creating possibilities with true insight,
knowing the outcome will be a delight.
Releasing all judgments that brought on the strife,
harmonizing all relationships for the rest of your life.

Follow this model so you can break the Code.
Pre-paving desires as you go up the road.

—Margaret McCraw
May 23, 2010

PART I

Insights Into Your Relationships

What Is the HARMONIC MATCHING PROCESS?

CHAPTER ONE

Pay less attention to what men say. Just watch what they do.
—Dale Carnegie

Many of us are seeking to connect with others. To attract desirable relationships in both the workplace and in our personal lives we must create a harmonic consciousness by sending out positive thoughts about ourselves and about others. What is consciousness? It is the combination of thoughts, emotions, and beliefs that make up our experiences. Although our consciousness is not tangible, we can see the result of what we are thinking, believing, and feeling by looking more closely at what we attract into our lives at any given moment. Any feelings we have of doubt or unworthiness can prevent us from having all we deserve. One thing is true and clear: We are all sending out vibrations through our consciousness. We cannot see the waves of energy we are sending out into the Universe; what we do see are the results of what we are projecting.

At one time it was believed that matter and energy were separate entities, but quantum physics has revealed that all matter, including every bird, flower, and human being, pulsates with energy. Even the smallest subatomic particles are not solid, but are actually compressed vibrating energy. Everything vibrates at its own unique frequency, creating what we perceive as light, color, heat, sound, electromagnetic fields, and solid matter.

MAGNETIC ATTRACTION

Our bodies have an electromagnetic frequency that responds to other vibrational frequencies. When two frequencies are attuned to each other, they are said to be in resonance with each other. In resonance, the vibratory source produces waves that impart energy to objects and other living things. If these objects, individuals, or other life forms have the same frequency, they will be set in motion. Resonance is the fundamental principle of the law of attraction, or "like attracts like," which is universal. In fact, when you strike the C string of an instrument such as a violin or a piano, all the other octave strings of C begin to vibrate even though you did not touch them. Although other strings may absorb the energy of the plucked string, only those with the same frequency are set in motion.

All of life is an interaction with the vibrational consciousness of others, which means we attract what we project into the world, as well as what we focus on. It is time to begin creating a harmonic consciousness in such a way that we radiate our true desires and attract endless possibilities within our own lives.

HARMONIC MATCHING

Harmonic Matching is the deliberate intention to attract our desires by aligning and focusing our thoughts, emotions, and beliefs with what we want rather than what we fear. In other words, it is drawing in a desired outcome by creating a vibrational consciousness that will resonate with our desires and bring it in. We are transmitting and receiving vibrations every moment of our lives. We always attract into our lives those things we resonate with, wanted or unwanted—things that vibrate at the same frequency as our consciousness. If you honestly want to rekindle a relationship, move up the corporate ladder, or reconnect with a long-lost friend, then you must begin by creating a vibrational consciousness that is in harmony with your desires. You do this by releasing fear and focusing on your desires; thereby, projecting vibrations at a higher, more loving frequency. When your thoughts are combined with intense positive feelings and emotions, they become powerful and enable you to align with your desires.

~~~

It is important to understand that our thoughts come first. It is equally important to realize that our emotions are a direct result of what we are thinking. This means we can take complete control of our feelings by changing what we think. Psychologists have just recently begun to understand this after much research on optimism and pessimism in the past 30 years. Positive emotion is an indicator that we are giving attention to what we desire, whereas negative emotion is an indicator that our thoughts are focused on the fear of not having what we want. Opening our minds to new beliefs will help us to create new thoughts, which is the key to emotional freedom.

What is your vibratory level at this time? Are your thoughts channeling powerfully positive vibrations to others seeking the same things you are seeking? Or are your thoughts laced with negatives like, "My boss doesn't notice anything I do," or "I'm just not good enough for her," or "My kids don't appreciate me." Even the smallest negative thought can disturb the resonance and create waves of discord. These lower vibrations can be felt in many different kinds of social dynamics.

You Can Only Love Others as Much as You Love Yourself

Desire is a strong wish, for something for which we long or hope. We have been taught to think about what is best for others and to exclude ourselves. We have learned to sacrifice ourselves, and so we give from a sense of obligation, not inspiration. This is especially true when it comes to our jobs. We go to work each day from a sense of obligation. We fear losing our sense of security, so we often stay in a job we detest in order to maintain a sense of comfort and familiarity.

Let's look at the dilemma Grace is facing and see how she finds resolutions to some of her challenges. Grace is a married woman and mother with two children at home. Like many working mothers, she works to give her family what they need to maintain the lifestyle to which they have grown accustomed. She works at a local bank, where she is in charge of the informational services division, a job that gives a fair income. But it is a demanding job. Many days, she works from morning to night, which leaves her very little time to spend with her husband and children. After a long day at work, she goes home weary and feeling a deep sense of emptiness.

Grace feels as though she is losing touch with family and friends. She also feels a sense of numbness, as if she were functioning more as a machine than a human being. She is losing herself. Even her coworkers are having difficulty seeing her as anything more than just the clichéd impersonal boss. Long gone are her days of enjoying a novel, riding a horse, or taking a ski weekend with friends on a beautiful mountaintop. Her life is now consumed by four office walls that seem to be closing in on her. She is surrounded by mounting paperwork, endless calls, dying plants, and frustrated employees who have lost respect for her because she has no time for them. Her temper has become short, and she has somehow lost her ability to mentor or lead her employees.

Finally, after her long annual review meeting with her boss, it all came crashing down on her. In the review, her boss cited reports from employees about her inability to lead others and emphasized her loss of focus on her work.

She left that meeting completely devastated. Then she became furious. "How dare he criticize my work when I've logged in more than 70 hours a week?!" After some more re-flection, however, Grace is forced to admit that her boss was right. In the past, she had enjoyed her work. Until recently, she had felt deeply respected by this same boss. It is now time for her to make changes in her life.

The very next day, Grace hires a life coach. This coach en-courages her to create a weekly schedule that includes much more time with her family, an exercise regime three morn-ings a week and once on the weekend, and leisure time each evening to read. She and her life coach work together to find ways to make this plan succeed. Next, Grace schedules another meeting with her boss in which they review her plan together. He supports her proposal and asks for only a few changes. This meeting alone gives Grace hope that she is indeed taking charge of her life again. It also gives her a renewed ambition to make the most of her time, not only at work but everywhere else in her life. She begins working fewer hours, but she seems to be more energetic and productive during those hours. She arrives home earlier and spends more time with her family. Helping her children with homework is fun again, and her husband feels a deeper sense of appreciation of her now that she is around more often.

At work, she forces herself to let go of some smaller tasks and begins delegating more of these to her assistant director. Soon she schedules a meeting with her team in which she apologizes for her short temper and acknowledges her lack of leadership. She asks them to submit ideas to her that will help create a more effective organization and a friendlier work culture. When her team's ideas are implemented, they save the division more than 20 overtime hours every month. She and her staff are working less, producing more, and saving money! This effort does not, of course, go unnoticed by her boss.

Grace no longer dreads going to work, and in showing consideration for herself, she is also able to show more for her employees. They are again willing to go the extra mile for her.

In addition, as they are allowed to show and use their own talents more as Grace gives up more control, her department initiates several new projects. The whole division begins to shine. They also initiate a wellness program that will eventually be implemented throughout the bank. Within a few years, Grace has moved from a place of desperation into a position of abundance. In addition she received a bonus that is large enough to hire an assistant, thus allowing her to be even more efficient.

What has Grace learned? She had to put herself and her needs first in order to find herself again. Although some people might call this selfishness, it is really living from integrity. This is the first and most critical component in being able to give to others.

~~~

How can we allow joy to fill our souls when we do not acknowledge our own desires? Desire lets the life force flow through us. Desire leads us to our life purpose. When you stop desiring, you lose your reason for living. If your heart is empty from not wanting anything, then that is exactly what you will get—*nothing*.

What We Focus on Becomes Our Reality

Here is another example of the importance of Harmonic Matching.

Lori feels that she has no real friends. She feels that people are taking advantage of her, that her friends are using her and lying to her. She says that all she wants is for her so-called friends to stop being disrespectful to her and treat her with the same level of integrity that she offers them. When they call her and need to talk about their problems, she always listens, and when they ask her to keep something confidential, she does so. She would never think about saying a word about their secrets to anyone. When they invite her out, she always says yes and never thinks about canceling. At the same time, however, she is convinced that these same friends only call her when they want something from her. When she tries to call one of them to talk about her life, they are nowhere to be found. They ignore her, brush her off when she wants to do something, and lie to her about their plans to avoid going to social events altogether. Lori needs to find a new set of friends. For some reason, however, whenever she makes new friends, this same pattern repeats itself.

Let's look more closely at how Lori handles her relationships. She seems to think the problem lies with her friends, that it has nothing to do with her. She begins all of her new relationships by venting about past friendships and telling horror stories about how her so-called friends ignored her, lied to her, used her, and borrowed money from her.

Here is Lori's problem: If she wants to attract different friends, she must understand that because she focuses attention on *what does not work* in her relationships, she just attracts more of the same. The more that she places her sense of well-being in the hands of others, the more insecure she becomes. Insecurity breeds fear and anxiety, which create barriers that block us from attracting good, supportive relationships. If Lori wants to attract better relationships, she will need to work with the Harmonic Matching Process. She will have to take the following steps:

× Be appreciative of what she has learned from her undesirable relationships.

× Allow the past to help her get clear about the type of friendship she wants to attract now.

× Focus her attention on *what she wants* instead of on the qualities of people who disappointed her. Given her history, she may want to set the intention to attract a new set of friends who:

• Genuinely like being with her.

• Balance giving and receiving.

- Are honest and loyal.
- Have a high level of integrity.
- Follow through with commitments.
- Are fun to be with.
- Appreciate and respect her.

× Allow herself to have fun while thinking, feeling, and fantasizing about her new group of friends. Visualize the fun things that she will be doing with them. Be lighthearted about all of this.

× Create time to do fun things by herself so that her happiness does not depend on someone or something outside of herself. In doing this, she will learn to appreciate herself and the difference between being alone and being lonely.

Lori's well-being depends solely on herself. She does not need to wait for others to come into her life in order to have fun. If we put our life on hold waiting for someone or something to come and make us happy, we delay the arrival of our desires. When we base our peace of mind or happiness on something else and put ourselves on hold for that something else to come to fruition, we are coming from a place of lack. The more Lori moves forward in a positive direction and allows herself to feel good about the new set of friends she intends to create, the faster she will attract new and positive relationships.

What we think and feel becomes our vibration. As we focus our attention on the thrill of achieving our desires, we come closer to having our dreams come true. As we likewise focus on our fear of not having what we want, we inhibit our desires from coming to fruition. We cannot fool the Universe by pretending to be something we're not. Like attracts like, and what we focus on becomes our reality.

~~~

Vibrations of similar frequencies are magnetized to each other. This magnetic force, this resonance, is what makes us the creator of our own world. What we love, we attract. But what we despise, we also attract. This is because we are projecting a consciousness of judgment, which means we are giving focused attention to something we do not desire. What we focus attention on shows up in our experience—positive or negative, just or unjust, passionate or dull, peaceful or chaotic. Whether we choose to believe it or not, we are forming our own destiny.

Whether the relationship you want to develop is in business connections or with friends, neighbors, or intimate partners, you can synchronize your life with ease and grace when you embrace three simple truths:

1. You have the ability to create your dreams at work and at home.

2. There is an abundance of options for every desire you have.

3. Truly loving yourself, coupled with gratitude, opens the doorway to prosperity of all kinds.

As you align with these simple truths, you set the stage to co-create a magnificent dance in your life, the dance of joy. Allow yourself to accept all of the possibilities that are out there waiting on you right now. They are intoxicating and irresistible. You deserve them!

Scarcity Consciousness Creates More Lack

It is important to understand that an "us versus them" mentality arises from scarcity consciousness. But our desires never have to interfere with someone else's well-being. Our happiness or sense of well-being never comes from another person, or, for that matter, from the fulfillment of a desire. Our well-being grows from knowing we are worthy of achieving our dreams. Our ability to attract, create, and receive depends on aligning our consciousness with the essence of our desires. Our well-being never comes from controlling others, allowing ourselves to be controlled, or desperately needing to have something (a partner, new boss, more money, and so on) in order to be happy. *This is scarcity*. Whenever you put your peace of mind or happiness on hold for something or someone to come into your life, or for someone to do something, then you are coming from a place of lack, and you are not in harmonic alignment with your desires.

Here is another example of how scarcity thinking can be overcome. Todd, age 28, works as an accountant at an investment firm. He began this job approximately three months ago, coming into the company with almost seven years of experience. His first three months at this company have been golden; his boss has seemed pleased with his work. Todd has been meeting deadlines and getting new clients. He feels that he is in a great position to advance in the firm if things continue to go smoothly throughout the next year.

After he passes his three-month probationary period, however, things begin to change. A new boss arrives. Suddenly the honeymoon is over. The new boss does not seem to be impressed with Todd's work, and he is no longer being invited out to lunch with the leadership team. One day, Todd approaches the new boss and asks if things are okay. He is stunned when the boss replies, in a kind by solemn voice, that he does not think Todd is a "good fit" with the firm.

Todd begins to feel that this is somehow personal. His fears grow as the days go by, and soon he is feeling great anger toward the boss. He desperately wants another new boss. But Todd's feelings of desperation are based on scarcity consciousness, and he does not see the options available to him. If he felt more secure, he might realize that he is not limited to working at that company. He might recognize that he has a marketable set of skills. If he felt better about himself, he might open himself up to an abundance of options. One option is addressing work issues with his new boss in an appropriate manner and attempting to understand what his boss is concerned about, with the intention to do better. He might learn to understand that doors often close because it is time for us to open ourselves to something different. It's true that when we feel good about ourselves, we recognize that we have many options. We can turn our focus to creating something new and better in our lives. If we open ourselves to our highest good and to the highest good of others, we are aligning with an abundance consciousness.

The essence of desire is passion. Allowing yourself to want something more, to believe in something beautiful, and to yearn for that feeling for the rest of your life is the first step to getting all you have always dreamed. Ask yourself these questions: *What do I want? How long has it been since I truly allowed myself the luxury of asking this question?*

Take a moment and just reflect on what you passionately want. Then take it a step further: Get out a sheet of paper or sit down at your computer and dare to write down your deepest desires. As you do this, be bold with the details. Describe specifically what you want from life. Write freely and withhold nothing. Describe everything you want. Tap into your poetic nature and give all the juicy details.

Now, after you have listed everything you desire, make another list or write another paragraph. This describes all you have to offer this world. Specific details at this stage are important, for you are beginning to redefine your state of mind and build a vision that will energize your thoughts and turn them into action. You may want to read this list or paragraph every day. Fantasize about your new life until you truly begin to feel the reality of it within your grasp. Your amazing life is out there already. It's waiting for you to make the decision that you are worthy of attracting the wonderful and ideal things you desire.

Stop denying yourself. Begin acknowledging your dreams. Begin fantasizing about your new life. It is through these powerful and repetitive positive feelings that you will attract your desires. Identifying what you want is only the first step. After that, you must align your thoughts, emotions, and beliefs to match the high frequency of your desires. Refer to Diagram 1-1 to more fully understand Harmonic Matching.

Diagram 1-1
Harmonic Matching

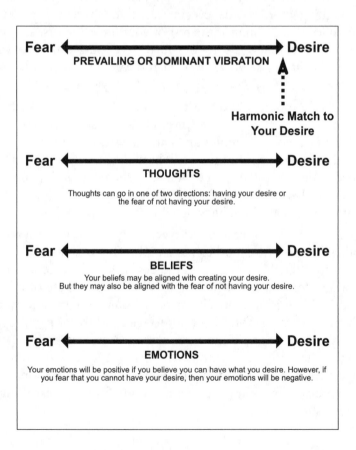

Fear ⟵————————————⟶ **Desire**
PREVAILING OR DOMINANT VIBRATION

Harmonic Match to
Your Desire

Fear ⟵————————————⟶ **Desire**
THOUGHTS
Thoughts can go in one of two directions: having your desire or
the fear of not having your desire.

Fear ⟵————————————⟶ **Desire**
BELIEFS
Your beliefs may be aligned with creating your desire.
But they may also be aligned with the fear of not having your desire.

Fear ⟵————————————⟶ **Desire**
EMOTIONS
Your emotions will be positive if you believe you can have what you desire. However, if
you fear that you cannot have your desire, then your emotions will be negative.

Is it really possible to align our desires with a consciousness of a higher frequency? *Yes, it is possible*. It is as simple as tuning your radio. To make this clearer, let's explore the concept of high-frequency radio waves. High-frequency radio waves allow radio operators to send signals over long distances, across oceans, and to other continents. Imagine setting your own frequency at a level so high that you can send signals anywhere and at any time. This requires you to tune in to your own waves of thoughts and emotions. Specifically, to reach a higher frequency, you must engage in the four-step Harmonic Matching Process:

1. Create feel-good moments.
2. Identify your desires.
3. Activate your intentions.
4. Release the outcome.

You will learn the specifics of how to embrace this four-step process in Part II of this book.

RESONANCE

Resonance occurs when two frequencies are attuned to each other, regardless of whether the vibration is high or low. When the vibration is high, we feel a strong emotional connection. It is as though someone is calling us. It is during these times that an immediate surge of positive energy flows within us. You feel a sense of harmony with something or someone outside yourself. When you learn to attune to these frequencies within your own physical being, you recognize that you have attracted someone who is responding to your desires. Or perhaps you are responding to the vibration of another. As you begin to correlate your thoughts, emotions, and beliefs with what you are attracting, you face each day with hope, optimism, and dynamic energy. You begin to create synchronicities in your life. The right people show up at just the right time.

Resonance can also occur when two lower vibrations align and cause stress, pain, and affliction. When we do not feel good about ourselves, we attract others who reinforce our beliefs of unworthiness. We see examples of this every day. Sometimes we see a couple spewing words of bitterness, disgust, competition, and anger at each other. Sometimes we see coworkers who belittle us in an effort to boost their own egos. Sometimes so-called friends send us negative messages that whisper of inadequacy to our inner beings. It is these situations, positive or negative, that reinforce our prevailing vibration. Unless we take responsibility for what we attract and consciously shift our thoughts, emotions, and beliefs about ourselves and our situations, we will attract repetitive situations with no end in sight.

I remember a mother and daughter for whom the resonance between them was so strong that it prevented both of them from feeling peace in other areas of their lives.

Amy, a successful woman of 36, believes that her mother was very controlling. She could not sit in the same room with her mother without being ordered around. "Why don't you pick up that laundry?" "Watch your language." "Go tell your father I need him." The demands went on and on.

With this model, Amy learned to be very controlling with her children, her coworkers, and her friends. Her friends have, in fact, nicknamed her "bossy," and her coworkers call her a control freak behind her back. She has the same traits as her mother, and when the two of them get together, it is as if war has been declared. Their conversations inevitably end with one slamming the phone down or walking out the door and slamming it behind her.

Amy and her mother have always resonated with each other. Neither of them can see it. They have no idea how much alike they are. Gaining insight into this unproductive alignment of energies is the first step they might take to move in a different direction.

Do you feel any positive or negative resonance within your circle of friends and family? If you do, and if you want to better understand what aspects of others you are resonating with, begin aligning your thoughts, emotions, and beliefs with what you are attracting. You can intentionally realign your vibrations. Resonance, both positive and negative, creates synchronicities in our lives where patterns repeat themselves. Nothing is coincidental.

SYNCHRONICITY AND OUR PREVAILING VIBRATION

Synchronicity occurs when frequencies align in such a way that a meaningful coincidence of two or more events occurs, where something other than the probability of chance is involved. Let me explain this by using Kim as an example. Kim, age 38, is dedicated to her daily exercise regimen. Every Tuesday, she walks along the same route from her house, through several neighborhoods, around a school, and onto a track. She walks the track, then turns around and heads back home. The walk is just over three miles, and she never veers a step from it.

One day, as she is walking near the school, something in her feels conflicted. She hesitates, just for a moment. "What an odd feeling," she says to herself. "I've been feeling completely positive, but now this bad energy has just come over me and I can't shake it." Honoring this feeling as meaningful, Kim alters her course and makes a right turn onto a different street. Within seconds, she hears a loud crash on the street she just left. She turns around to see what happened. A large truck, suddenly out of control, has just crashed into the curb with enough speed and force to cross the sidewalk. If Kim had stayed on her usual course, she would have been run over by the truck.

Now some might dismiss this event as a mere coincidence. But let me continue. As Kim walks back to the scene to check on the driver, she discovers that the man was an old friend. They lost contact when his career took him to another state.

And now here they are, reunited in this moment that could have been a tragedy. By acting on her intuition, Kim not only spared herself a possibly critical accident, but she has also reconnected with a dear friend she lost track of years ago.

To better understand how this synchronistic event occurred, let's take a look at Kim's prevailing vibration. Overall, she has a very strong sense of well-being. She loves her work as a nurse and feels a strong sense of passion and purpose in it. In general, you might say that she flows with her life, and on those occasions when something goes off kilter, she remains optimistic and resilient and keeps on truckin'. When the accident occurred, therefore, she had a longstanding history of being an optimist with a prevailing vibration of well-being.

Synchronistic resonance happens in an unexplainable instant in a seemingly random moment when everything appears to come together. What are prevailing vibrations, and how do they create synchronistic events? Persistent thoughts and beliefs about ourselves in conjunction with strong emotion make up the prevailing vibrational consciousness that magnetizes our relationships. The stronger and more positive our prevailing vibration is about a particular desire, the more quickly we will become a harmonic match to it. The stronger and more negatively charged we are about something we do not desire, the more quickly we will attract what we do *not* want. There are three components to creating our prevailing vibration:

1. The intensity and the clarity of our desire.
2. The strength of our belief associated with our desire.
3. The feeling tone associated with our desire.

Clarity plus our level of enthusiasm for our desire equals the intensity of our desire. For example, how important is it to you to attract a relationship, such as a new business partner?

The feeling tone, which can be positive or negative, is the intensity of the passion associated with a particular desire. For example, you might express a positive feeling tone in this way: "I'm so excited that my new boss appreciates me. She told me she wouldn't want anyone else but me working on this project with her. Hooray!"

Belief is also a factor in whether or not the feeling tone is positive or negative. If our belief that we can have what we want is strong, then the feeling tone is more likely to be positive. If our belief is weak, then our feeling tone is more likely to be negative. If, for example, a woman tells her best friend, "I really want my children to admire me, but they will never respect me. They never listen to what I say," her feeling tone is negative and translates into a low frequency.

~~~

When we are not aware of our persistent thoughts and what we are giving attention to, we are *unconsciously* creating our prevailing vibration. When we are aware of our thoughts, beliefs, corresponding emotions with regard to ourselves, and desires, then we are *consciously* creating our prevailing vibration. Part II of this book teaches you how to consciously attract the relationships you want by creating a vibrational consciousness that is in harmony with your desires. Becoming aware of your thoughts, beliefs, and corresponding emotions—as you correlate them with the experiences you are attracting—is a prerequisite for consciously creating your desired relationships with family, friends, coworkers, bosses, and others.

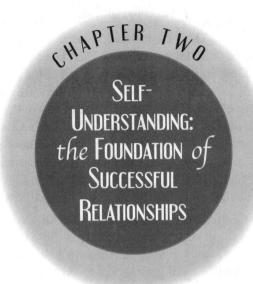

CHAPTER TWO

SELF-UNDERSTANDING: the FOUNDATION of SUCCESSFUL RELATIONSHIPS

Know thyself.
—The Oracle at Delphi

Even though our relationships at work and at home can sometimes be challenging, people are strongly motivated to be with others. To better understand our relationships, we have to look within.

UNDERSTANDING INTUITION AND SELF-LOVE

Before we can build a positive relationship with ourselves, we first need to understand more about our own motivators; that is, what we want and what we avoid. You can gain deeper self-understanding and self-love by looking within.

The word *intuition* comes from the Latin word *intueri*, which means "to look within," "to contemplate," or "to regard inwardly." As you spend more time with yourself, you can learn to become a better friend to yourself. When you pay attention to your inner feelings, you can strengthen your intuitive abilities. This attention ultimately impacts the decisions you make on a day-to-day basis. As the renowned Swiss psychiatrist Dr. Carl Jung indicated in much of his work, intuitive knowledge comes to us from the collective consciousness of the Universe, which we all have the ability to access when we quiet the busy chatter in our minds and open ourselves to the highest good of all concerned. This kind of knowledge can lead to enormously beneficial guidance in all aspects of our lives. It especially helps us gain greater self-understanding and encourages us to allow the growth of healthy self-love.

Intuition, which opens us to better relationships and new opportunities in all aspects of our lives, is the natural faculty of the soul that allows higher guidance to help us. When we develop the habit of paying attention to our small, soft, inner voice or feeling, our intuition can be our compass, our warning system, and our guide to great positive opportunities. It operates as a wonderful support in our lives.

Imagine that you could not see, and then someone showed you how you could develop sight. What a wonderful new power you would have. By increasing your understanding of yourself and your motivators, you can awaken a channel to enhance relationships of all kinds, discover new business opportunities, and nourish your whole life.

Self-Love

How can we love others if we do not love ourselves? How can we love ourselves if we do not get to know ourselves? Healthy self-love is not the same thing as being selfish or conceited. Self-love means coming to peace with yourself and allowing yourself to grow.

Compassionate self-understanding leads to self-love and establishes a strong foundation for positive relationships with others. By letting go of self-criticism, we become open to the adventure of life and the potential for new experiences. We are also much less apt to be critical of others and more able to develop compassion for those at work and in our personal circle.

CONSCIOUS AND SUBCONSCIOUS MOTIVATORS

To better understand ourselves in the context of our relationships, we need to look at the motivators that draw us into relationships with others. When you ask yourself what you want from a relationship, you can gain greater understanding, and greater ability to get the things you want. In the process, you will also come to understand other people better.

Some of these motivators are close enough to the surface of our mind that we can easily "see" them. We can refer to these as *conscious motivators*. Others are more deeply buried in the subconscious. By using your intuitive guidance to look more closely at your buried motivators, you can bring them into conscious awareness where you can work with them.

Conscious Motivators in Relationships

When you are conscious of the desires that are motivating you in relationships, you can see more clearly what you want from the people you interact with, both at home and at work. This allows you to build strong intentions for successful relationships, and helps you see when they are not working and what you can do about it.

Here are six factors that motivate us to seek and stay in relationships:

1. Companionship.
2. Validation.
3. Care, love, and intimacy.
4. Connection.
5. Co-creation.
6. Mentoring.

Companionship has to do with having resonance with someone; sharing what you like to do. Validation comes when other people affirm your value. Though we cherish being validated, it is good to develop your own self-validation that is not dependent on others. All of us need love and care; sometimes more than others. The more we love and understand ourselves, the more we will be open to intimacy with those special others we have come to trust. Sharing our truth with intimate others is helpful in having successful relationships.

Connection has to do with wanting to feel we are part of a larger mission, vision, or purpose. Relationships in organizations need to be built on clearly communicating the big picture and where everyone fits into it. When people in an organization do not understand what all the other parts of the organization do, and how they personally fit into the process, they will feel disconnected. Everyone wants to know how they fit in.

When I was consulting for a large organization, its leadership asked me to do a culture analysis for them. One of the key issues that emerged was that people didn't know one another because of the complexity and geographic dispersal of the organization. Even with e-mail, telephone, video conferencing, and other technological means of connection, people were not feeling actually connected. This was causing the organization to suffer in productivity, in personnel retention, and in all aspects of efficiency and effectiveness. I helped them understand that their mission and purpose had to be defined in ways that could be understood on all levels, from the boardroom down to the front line. I helped employees see how their day-to-day jobs fit into the bigger picture. The result was measurable improvement as the organization began to work better and become an integrated whole. This example shows how the connection motivator can work for or against successful relationships, depending on how well it is addressed.

Co-creation refers to our desire to work creatively with others and the satisfaction that comes from sharing and teamwork. (This is described more fully in Chapter 3.) Another important factor we consciously seek in relationships is mentoring. We gain confidence and skills by interacting with more experienced people who are willing to share their knowledge, guidance, and encouragement with us so we can grow and learn. Those who mentor feel valued and emotionally rewarded for their knowledge and expertise.

Subconscious Factors in Relationships

As we come to know ourselves better, we discover motivators that are hidden in our subconscious. Even though you may not have been aware of these motivators until now, they are still controlling many of the patterns you see in your relationships. By making them conscious, you gain the ability to transform them into something more positive.

The subconscious and the ego keep us locked into old patterns of behaviors. Here are some motivators and needs that may be subconsciously influencing your relationships:

- ✗ Need for control.
- ✗ Need to be approved of.
- ✗ Need to be liked.
- ✗ Need to be admired.
- ✗ Need to be rewarded.
- ✗ Need to maintain the status quo, or familiar situation.
- ✗ Need to feel good about ourselves.
- ✗ Need to reinforce a particular identity.

What we believe about ourselves and others becomes the subconscious force that conditions all our relationships. If our thoughts, emotions, and beliefs are in alignment with our true desires, our subconscious works on our behalf to create these intentions. If there is significant resistance of any kind, such as worry or fear associated with achieving our desires, the subconscious will help us attract what we are giving focused attention to, regardless of whether it is our desire or our fear of not having what we want in our life. The subconscious does not recognize or categorize our desires as "good" or "bad." It simply helps us attract what we believe about ourselves and others.

The Self-Fulfilling Prophecy Really Exists

Here's an example. Sam had what he perceived as very bad experience with a female boss when he was hired right out of college by an engineering firm. He felt his boss did not trust him, and micromanaged him on a day-to-day basis. He soon left this job to accept a position in another company. He was thrilled that his new boss was a man, someone with whom he had worked previously, and, he felt, really liked him. Three weeks later, however, his boss was promoted and re-located to another state. Sam's new boss was a woman who expected him to prove his worth by submitting endless reports justifying everything he was doing. Sam soon left this job to work elsewhere. Once again, he was reporting to a man. Three months later, this company merged with a larger corporation, and once again Sam was reporting to a woman he considered to be a tyrant, always putting him down in front of others, and demoting him to a lesser position in the company.

As you can see, in Sam's life there was an endless string of repeated circumstances in which, no matter how hard he tried to create what he thought he wanted, he consistently attracted what he feared. His subconscious did not judge one set of circumstance as good or bad; it simply assisted him in attracting situations that affirmed his belief about women—that they were bad bosses. The only way Sam could attract something different was to stop judging women and be open to seeing them as being good leaders. But if Sam makes this change, it will require conscious effort on his part to look beyond his set of circumstances and be willing to acknowledge the fact that not all women are tyrants or micromanagers. In doing so, Sam will release some of his fears and judgments and become open to attracting a boss he perceives as helpful and supportive. The more Sam is willing and open to consciously create a new belief system about women as leaders, the greater the chance that he will attract the outcome he wants, which is to feel good about his relationship with the person who oversees his work.

Set your intentions to learn your lessons gently.
—Anonymous Proverb

~~~

Let us look at the need to reinforce a particular identity. People are mentally and emotionally aligned with justifying what they *think* is their reason for existence. For example, our jobs exist because people need our services. If for any reason this need no longer exists, then we may feel our jobs are threatened, which may cause us to foster dependence rather than seeing the people we serve from a place of well-being.

If we feel secure in ourselves, we become free to discover new reasons for existing that may be even more interesting and satisfying than what we are familiar with. People who have greater self-understanding tend to be more secure and more willing to share information rather than hoarding it. By not clinging to a narrow idea of how to live your mission or reason for being, you can line up with new opportunities for greater fulfillment, either inside the organization or outside it. When we are aligned to opportunity, this can become a win/win for people coming and going from an organization, and for the highest good of the organization as well.

When people have a sense of their own personal vision and how it relates to their work in an organization, they are more resilient and better able to flex with the ups and downs of their jobs. For example, I was hired as a consultant to a large health-care organization to address the culture and advise its leaders on ways to enhance staff retention while creating a more committed workforce. During my interview with the director of training, it became apparent to me that he was unhappy in his current position. He wanted to write books and be a keynote speaker. He had a message that he wanted to communicate to the world. When he told me that he was not happy there and that he wanted to quit his job, I asked him some questions to help him understand where he was with this vision:

"Do you feel ready to be a keynote speaker? Do you believe you can get a job as a keynote speaker? Is your message developed? Are you happy with it?"

"Hold a vision of where you want to be," I told him. "Now, let's talk about timing. Who do you see hiring you right now to give a keynote speech? You need to believe that you are worth it. You need to be confident that this is your value."

Knowing that the self-fulfilling prophecy is real (that what we believe about ourselves and the world around us is indeed what we attract), I was assessing his mental and emotional readiness for living his dream: If this man quits his job now, is he in alignment to get a better position in the next four weeks?

He wasn't.

Then I asked, "Why quit now? Do you feel there are things in this job that can help you prepare to live your dream? What greater way to position yourself to be an author and a keynote speaker than to bring in trainers in your current job and learn from them what works well and what doesn't? You can gain a wealth of knowledge for your intended future career."

The reason I asked these questions and made these suggestions was that I saw that although he had a vision for his future, he needed to build the staircase that would align him with his intention (refer to Figure 7-1 in Chapter 7 to better understand this concept). What I was doing in this five-minute conversation was helping this man make the inner connection with his life purpose, or vision, and see the gifts of where he was right now in his present job.

Part of being in a successful relationship is being connected to yourself and your life purpose or vision. Even if you are not clear about this, you can begin by making a statement about how you want to walk through life. This is your first step in moving forward in a positive direction.

WHY WE ATTRACT UNDESIRABLE RELATIONSHIPS

One of the main reasons we attract undesirable relationships is that they fulfill our subconscious need for familiar situations that are in alignment with beliefs we hold about ourselves and others. The patterns we have learned from our family of origin and our past experiences with relationships have developed ingrained habits in us that are much like bad programming in our mental computer.

The subconscious is a very dutiful servant. No matter what messages we send to it, this servant works to fulfill. By looking within and getting to know yourself better, you can see how you are calling for things you do not consciously want. You can develop greater self-love, learn to have compassion for why you are at times attracting painful and unpleasant relationships, and decide to create something better. You can become a better friend to yourself.

When we understand the motivators that are attracting undesirable relationships, we can see them as gifts to help us grow and align ourselves to attract positive relationships.

Whatever the mind...can conceive and believe, it can achieve.
—Napoleon Hill

The "conceive" part of Hill's statement tells us that we can use deliberate, conscious thought to define our intentions. The "believe" part tells us that we must align our thoughts and emotions with a positive outcome and convince our subconscious that we really mean to make a change.

HOW WE SET OURSELVES UP FOR NEGATIVE OUTCOMES

Consider this story of a talented young man who set himself up for a negative outcome:

John, a project manager in the software development division of a large corporation, was very interested in the creative aspects of interactive video production. But his father was a retired executive who had always looked down on John's creative interests and wanted him to follow in his footsteps to upper management. John's supervisors were impressed with his skills and offered him a director position where he would be mentored by the chief information officer. Because the money was good and John craved the approval of his mentor, he accepted the position. Very soon, however, he realized that his new job called for little of the creative energy he truly loved. His mentor was also proving to be demanding and critical, much like his father. John felt as though his life was becoming empty, and, although he had the ability to do the job, his performance began to slip, making him liable to be criticized by important people. Soon he was feeling a growing resentment toward his mentor, who had taken the place of his father in his subconscious mental pattern. His subconscious need to be independent from his father was sabotaging his relationship with his new boss. Eventually, John blew up, re-creating a scene of teenage rebellion. He stayed on for a time, but a negative outcome was inevitable.

After he found greater understanding of his patterns, John joined a small interactive video company as a partner and a creative director. Here he was able to fulfill his creative desires and show his father that he had executive capability at the same time. The negative outcome and the pattern that led to it were transformed, freeing John from unnecessary emotional pain.

How We Inhibit Relationships and How to Let Go

Acting out negative emotions, aggressively or passively, is one of the primary ways we inhibit relationships. By looking within, we can come to understand what we are feeling and reduce the stress of keeping these emotions hidden from ourselves.

Greater understanding and compassion for yourself can help you avoid acting out, without repressing the truth of what you are feeling.

When we learn to stop acting out negative patterns, we free ourselves from unnecessary and painful dramas in our relationships that only take us away from understanding our true feelings. By working inwardly, we can understand why we are experiencing these patterns. In the logic of the subconscious, they always serve a purpose, even if we are not conscious of that purpose. By exploring our old patterns, we can make conscious decisions to create new patterns that will nourish desirable relationships instead of inhibiting them.

Here are some of the thought patterns that inhibit our work and personal relationships, often causing unnecessary loss:

- ✕ Pessimism.
- ✕ Criticism.
- ✕ Control.
- ✕ Sacrifice.
- ✕ Right/wrong thinking.
- ✕ Arguments.
- ✕ Dishonesty.
- ✕ Making excuses.

You can let go of inhibiting patterns by consciously setting the intention to become more self-aware and to release thoughts and beliefs that no longer serve you. For example, you may have developed a habit of pessimism to avoid being disappointed. Every pattern exists because it seemed to make sense at the time it was laid down. To release an undesirable pattern, simply set an intention of what you want and command your subconscious mind to help you attract your new desire. Remember, the subconscious mind is a servant to the conscious mind. For instance, if you want to release pessimism from your outlook, you could set the intention to be optimistic. To release a pattern of right/wrong thinking, you could set the intention to be open-minded and compassionate. So when you make this effort from a clear intention, you will replace negative patterns with a positive pattern, leading to more desirable outcomes. By letting go of these inhibitors, you are opening the door to delicious feelings of well-being and fresh new capacities to relate to others.

GIVING LOVINGLY VERSUS SACRIFICIAL GIVING

Do you believe that giving love has to hurt? Or do you believe that an overflowing heart gives naturally and joyously? Whatever you believe will be what you experience in your life. The Universe mirrors your consciousness back to you.

> *Remember happiness doesn't depend upon who you are or what you have; it depends solely on what you think.*
> —Dale Carnegie

We also are called upon to give a type of love in the workplace as well as in our personal lives. When we believe that giving love must be a sacrifice, we are choosing to believe that love is not abundant. We are choosing to align with a consciousness of scarcity, and so that will be true for us. However, this is a *choice*. You can *choose* to believe that love is abundant and freely available to everyone (even those who annoy and frustrate you). Choosing abundant love will fill your life with love. Remember, what we believe about ourselves and others is what we create.

We may think that self-love is the same thing as being selfish or narcissistic. Actually, the opposite is true. It is the *absence* of true self-love that makes us greedy to fill the lack within us. It is when we do not feel worthy that we pump ourselves up with egotistical displays. Sacrificial "love" is motivated by wanting to feel worthy, but it almost inevitably turns into resentment that our sacrifice is not sufficiently appreciated. It can even turn into hatred for the person we intended to love. True self-love, by contrast, fills us up with contentment and overflows toward everyone around us. We can listen to others when we are not so hungry for approval from them. We have enough love to give away.

When you gain deeper self-understanding and self-love, you can open the inner source of love. Take a moment to thank yourself for surviving and growing up to be who you are today. The fact that you are reading this book means that you are ready to explore these issues, which will lead to greater joy and abundance in your life.

When you fill your heart with love and appreciation for all the good things in your life, you begin to fill up from within. You can even feel gratitude for the challenges life has given you because these challenges become opportunities to acquire new strengths. As your heart fills up, you begin to change old patterns. You do not have to accept the old patterns; you can choose to change them by focusing on your desires, rather than your fears, and in doing so attract and create better relationships in all areas of your life, both personal and professional.

As you come into greater self-love, you will be able to give lovingly, not sacrificially. True self-love fills you with an abundant supply of love that you can share with others. This is the foundation of truly successful relationships at home and at work.

TOOLBOX FOR BUILDING POSITIVE RELATIONSHIPS

Here is a toolbox of resources you can use to shift from negative patterns of behavior to productive ways of connecting with others. These are the powerful tools that guide you on the path to developing a true connection to the love and joy within you, and that build positive relationships both at home and at work. You can also use these tools to create a more positive relationship with yourself.

15 Relationship Enhancers

1. Self-love.

2. Lightheartedness.

3. Enthusiasm.

4. Appreciation.

5. Encouragement.

6. Genuine interest.

7. Follow-through.

8. Generosity.

9. Optimism.

10. Seeing the best in others.

11. Seeing things from another's perspective.

12. Open-mindedness.

13. Integrity.

14. Respect.

15. Forgiveness and compassion.

When you make a sincere intention to develop any of these enhancers, you will start to attract the thoughts and feelings that will help you develop them into positive habitual patterns in your life. You can intentionally choose to seek these good qualities and build them up until they become part of your character. Because every person is different, some of these enhancers will come more easily to you than others. Start with those that come easiest. As you do so, you will become more open and optimistic, enabling you to attract the insight and understanding you need to develop even the qualities you had trouble with at first. Each level of success encourages you to reach for more, and all of these enhancers offer infinite depths of benefit. The more you make these enhancers part of your life, the more positive relationships and opportunities you will attract. You can even use these enhancers to attract the ability to overcome any resistances you discover within yourself.

Love is a state of mind that is fostered and re-created when you truly love yourself. **Self-love** is the powerful launching pad from which we attract positive relationships. It is reflected internally through having a strong sense of security and well-being, regardless of what is happening externally—if we feel loving toward ourselves, we attract others who feel the same way about us; if we feel unloving, fearful, or needy, we attract relationships that reinforce this vibration within us.

All relationships are improved when we approach them with **lightheartedness**. This enhancer takes the heaviness out of everything we do. You can choose to focus on being light-hearted and relaxed about life. Intentionally build up your **enthusiasm** for life. Develop your **appreciation** and gratitude for yourself and for all the people who come into your life. Who is not attracted by appreciation? Give **encouragement** to yourself and those you live and work with. Show **genuine interest** in others and train yourself to listen with a new ear and look with a kinder eye.

In all your relationships, including that with yourself, build trust by **following through** on your promises, and remind yourself not to over-promise. People are happier when you are honest with them about what you can and cannot deliver. When you have promised, do your best to over-deliver. This is also a way to bring **generosity** into all your relationships.

Optimism is the natural orientation when you believe that the world is abundant with all you need to fulfill your wishes. When you believe that good things are possible, and even probable, you attract them into your life. Optimism is contagious. Look to **see the best in others** and that is what they will bring you. Whatever comes, start with the assumption that other people want to bring forth their best. If you believe it, they may believe it too, and may surprise even themselves.

It is the great power of wise people to **see things from the perspective of others**. Try this: Sit quietly with your eyes closed and imagine that your mind has temporarily left your personality behind in your chair. Imagine that you can feel what it is like to be someone else you know, that you can almost become them for a little while. See things from their point of view and consider what would make them happier, what would elevate them on an emotional level. This is one of the best ways to clarify a relationship by deeper understanding. To do this requires **open-mindedness** to a perspective that is not your own normal way of looking at things. You may discover some wonderful opportunities you might not otherwise have seen.

Do you want to feel whole? The complexities of life and the many relationships that pull us and push us in different directions may leave us feeling fragmented. We may have to be one way at work, another way at home, and a completely different way with friends. Developing **integrity** means finding the common ground of our core beliefs and bringing that into all parts of our life. It not only helps us feel whole, but others will also see us as stronger, more congruent, and more solid, because that's what we are.

One key to **respect** comes from the humble realization that we don't know everything about another person (or even about ourselves). When we realize that every human being has vast potentials, whether they have ever shown them or not, it becomes natural to extend respect to them. Of course, common sense tells us that people respond better when we show them respect than when we don't.

The more open we are to **forgiving** everyone and everything, the lighter we will feel. Forgiveness is a gift to ourselves, not to the person we forgive. No matter what someone has done, if we can forgive and let go we will feel lighter. Forgiveness in the workplace is equally important as it is in our personal relationships. When we forgive our bosses, our coworkers, and our employees, we stop being the victim and replace powerlessness with being in control of our destinies. On the other hand, when we hold on to our judgments, we set ourselves up to attract more reasons to feel wronged by the same or other people. Remember, a key purpose of the subconscious is to affirm our beliefs about ourselves and others. If we believe we have been mistreated, and we give attention and negative emotion to this so-called mistreatment, then we will set ourselves up to create a pattern of being victimized. However, if we can acknowledge our feelings and yet choose to see the situation with compassion rather than judgment, we will align with well-being and attract more reasons to feel good.

Compassion is a deep well from which we can drink for the rest of our lives and never come to the bottom. True compassion allows us to know and empathize with another's pain while sustaining our own positive perspective. In companies at which I have consulted, I have seen the boss's compassion and forgiveness spread like a healing balm on an entire organization. But compassion does not mean being a self-sacrificing doormat; it guides us to lift others up rather than going down to meet them at a lower state.

If you embrace them, these enhancers can transform every aspect of your life. They can add to the bottom line, as well as motivate others to help you achieve your goals.

Assess Your Current State

Part of getting to know and love yourself better is becoming comfortable with the truth about where you are at any moment as you move forward on the path to self-knowledge. Be compassionate with yourself as you do this assessment. Remember, just as your beliefs formed your current state, new beliefs can create a new state at a higher level. The first step is to assess where you are in this present moment.

Using this scale, rate each of the following 15 items from 1 to 5, where:

> (1) indicates Never
> (2) indicates Rarely
> (3) indicates Sometimes
> (4) indicates Frequently
> (5) indicates All the Time

How often do you:

1. Spend quiet time alone with yourself, looking within and using your intuition to gain self-understanding?
Rating (1–5): _____

2. Check in with others whose opinions you trust to get an outside view about yourself?
Rating (1–5): _____

3. Respond with compassion instead of judgment to what you learn about yourself?
Rating (1–5): _____

4. Step back from difficult relationships and try to see them from an objective point of view rather than only from your own perspective?
Rating (1–5): _____

5. Perceive situations as unique, rather than label them as right or wrong?
Rating (1–5): _____

6. Set intentions to align with well-being, instead of focusing on your fears about any given situation?
Rating (1–5): _____

7. Choose to focus attention on the gifts in your life rather than giving attention to the things that don't feel good?
Rating (1–5): _____

8. Maximize your good qualities by focusing on them when you feel down, rather than minimizing your good qualities by berating yourself?
Rating (1–5): _____

9. Step back from your emotions when you receive feedback that feels negative, rather than becoming angry and defensive?
Rating (1–5): _____

10. Focus on the positive qualities of all people, regardless of whether you like them?
    Rating (1–5): _____

11. Learn from "mistakes" rather than blaming yourself or others?
    Rating (1–5): _____

12. Look for positive outcomes in unexpected and challenging situations rather than fearing the worst?
    Rating (1–5): _____

13. Gather complete information about what appear to be negative circumstances rather than taking statements or events out of context?
    Rating (1–5): _____

14. Replace *should*, *must*, and *ought* statements (which eliminate options) with *could*, *might consider*, and *perhaps* statements (which create options)?
    Rating (1–5): _____

15. Replace *why* statements with *help me to understand* statements, which shift from a perspective of defensiveness to gathering information or knowledge?
    Rating (1–5): _____

Score Yourself

71–75:	Extremely enhancing
61–70:	Very enhancing
51–60:	Usually enhancing
40–50:	Middle ground—sometimes enhancing and sometimes inhibiting
30–39:	Usually inhibiting
20–29:	Very inhibiting
15–19:	Extremely inhibiting

Regardless of your score, cultivating an optimistic attitude toward all areas of your life will enhance your ability to gain greater self-understanding and self-love. Be compassionate and nonjudgmental toward yourself. By being honest with yourself, you have taken a step toward greater integration and insight into who you are and what you want to become. The more positive your thoughts, the more quickly your desires will be manifested in your personal life and on your job.

EXERCISES

1. Set aside quiet time to be with yourself. Find ways to get comfortable with being alone with yourself. If you do not find that meditation, or simply sitting quietly, comes easily to you, you might start with some other type of relaxing activity. Engage in any activity that allows you to think and explore your feelings (not reading, watching TV, or talking). Spend time learning how to become your own best friend. Ask yourself questions such as these: "What do I want? What do I like? What makes me happy?" Your answers will help you to create more desirable outcomes in all areas of your life.

2. Take notes on your life. Keep a journal or a notebook where you write down what you want in your life. The more you focus attention on good feelings and the situations that you associate with good feelings, the more you will attract those kinds of energies, and your ability to create positive outcomes will rise to a new level.

3. Pick three relationship enhancers from the toolbox that you feel most comfortable with. Write them down in your notebook. Think about ways you can apply them to your relationships today. How can you apply them to your relationship with yourself, in relationships at home, and in relationships at work? Keep notes about

how your work with these relationship enhancers is going. What is working well? What is not? Sustain your optimism and intentionally encourage yourself. Reward yourself in simple ways as you progress.

Six Ways to Empower Others to Succeed

As this chapter has shown, understanding and loving ourselves puts us in a much better place to empower others to be successful. By learning the code of our own motivators, we gain the inner strength to get out of the way and engage others in a more responsive and loving way.

Here are six ways we can engage others and empower them (with their consent):

1. Ask what they want.
2. Listen.
3. Give helpful feedback.
4. Encourage.
5. Support.
6. Give an outside view.

This list does not mean that we can always give others what they want—often we can't, especially in the workplace. We can listen, however, and give the needed feedback, encouragement, and support so that other options become viable. As we empower others to succeed, we are seen by them and others as an ally. We are given more respect as we assist, mentor, and coach others to find solutions to thorny problems.

Through self-knowledge, we become more receptive to the powerful wisdom that is all around us. By learning to empower others, we also learn to love and empower ourselves more fully. Now take this knowledge into Chapter 3 as you learn to consistently co-create desirable outcomes with others.

CHAPTER THREE

Co-Create With Others

Self-expression must pass into communication for its fulfillment.
—Pearl S. Buck

Relationships are, at their core, about teamwork. Whether it is personal or professional relationships we are talking about—friendships, partnerships, familial relationships, or relating to coworkers or bosses—there is a joint effort underlying the spirit of the relationship. At least, that's the ultimate goal. When any two or more people come together, there are usually goals involved—to have fun, share an experience, give and receive help, or resolve a conflict. Hopefully, the goals are aimed at the mutual benefit of everyone involved. Sometimes, though, each person in the relationship has a different agenda. That is when conflict arises. Our energies come into play, often without our even knowing it, and either help or hinder our ability to successfully co-create and reach positive outcomes with others.

What is co-creating? Co-creating is the coming together of two or more people to reach a goal, find a solution, create

69

something new, or form a new bond. When two friends come together to see a movie or go to dinner, they may be attempting to co-create a stronger bond of love. They are co-creating a friendship. When coworkers come together, they are co-creating products or services. The more in synch everyone involved can be through the Harmonic Process, the more easily the co-creation will flow.

Harmonic Matching can be used across all relationships, both professional and personal, to help us co-create goals and make the most out of the connections we forge. What does communication have to do with co-creation? How do you successfully co-create? How is your vibrational consciousness level interacting with the vibrational levels of others in your efforts to co-create?

Here is an exercise to help you examine your communication style. Choose (a) or (b) from the following three scenarios:

1. A coworker sends you a file that you need in order to complete a project, but the file seems incomplete. You don't feel you have enough information to get the job done right, but you know your coworker is already working on another project. You:

    a. Say nothing and make do with what you have. You can piece something together and, if push comes to shove, you'll speak up later.

    b. Approach your co-worker and say, "I don't have all the information I need in order to complete the project. Is there any more information I can get from you? Is there some way we can work on this together?"

2. During a team meeting, someone brings up an issue with something you worked on recently. They give a critique of your work, and you respond by saying:

    a. "I think you're wrong, and here's why."

    b. "I understand what you're saying. This was my original reasoning, but I can see how it might not have come across that way. Any suggestions for how I might do it better?"

3. Your best friend asks for your help with a project. You are barely juggling your current schedule, and you know one more project will throw you into overload. You say:

   a. "Sure!" And you hang up the telephone feeling a lot of anxiety about your growing to-do list.

   b. "I'm currently having some difficulty managing my commitments. I want to help you find a solution, though. Can we work on this next month after I take care of my current commitments? Or is there someone else who may be in a position to help you right now?"

If you selected (b) in these examples, then you are in alignment with some of the communication "do's" listed in the following pages. Let us review some of the key ways in which we can optimally co-create with others, and in doing so align our consciousness to attract what we desire.

COMMUNICATION DO'S FOR OPTIMAL CO-CREATING AND HARMONIC MATCHING

Everything you bring into your experience comes to you because you are in vibrational harmony with it. You are thus a harmonic match for everything you attract, whether it is desirable or undesirable. You are a match because you have consciously or unconsciously given focused attention to something or because you have not set clear intentions around a particular desire. When you go through life without clear intentions, you attract a whole range of circumstances—some wanted, but many of them unwanted. By clarifying your desires, aligning your beliefs with them, and trusting in yourself, you can become the creator of your reality.

The following is a list of communication do's to enhance your relationships:

- × **Know what outcome you desire in every interaction.** We communicate as a means to achieve a desire. Desire is what makes the life force flow. Sometimes we are aware of our desires, but sometimes we are not. Communication is much more successful when we are clear about what we want.

- × **Understand that stating an intention is just the beginning of attracting what you want.** You must match your thoughts, beliefs, and emotions (your vibrational consciousness) with your desires. Even though strong, clear, desire coupled with strong be-lief that you can have what you want creates intention, your consciousness may contradict your intention. Intentions are a component of vibrational conscious-ness, but they are *not* synonymous with it. You will attract according to your vibrational alignment. For example, your intention may be to attract a new job with an income that is double your current position. If you do not believe that this is possible, however, your vibration will be in harmony with your current salary, rather than the salary of your desires. That means you will attract according to your vibrational offering.

- × **Be selective about your words and thoughtful in the tone you use to speak them aloud.** Your words and the tone of your voice carry a vibration. Thoughtfulness enables us to align our vibrational consciousness with our desire and attract what we want more easily. When we are thoughtful, we are aligned with well-being. When we are hurried or feeling stressed, on the other hand, the tone of our voice may be brash.

- × **Take responsibility for your feelings.** No one but you can make you feel good or bad. Only you are respon-sible for how you feel. When you say, "You make me feel [in such a way]," you are projecting a vibrational consciousness of powerlessness. No one else can make you feel anything. When you project powerlessness, you will attract more experiences aligned with feeling victimized. However, when you say, "I feel this way when you do this or that," you are projecting a vibration of taking charge. You will attract more experiences aligned with feeling in control of your life because you are taking responsibility for how you feel.

✕ **Co-create with integrity.** Be honest and true to yourself in all of your interactions. Establish clarity about what is important to you. Set intentions that your communication and interactions will be aligned with your values and of the highest degree of integrity.

✕ **Allow your communication to be inspired.** We always want to feel good. Let yourself be inspired into attracting feel-good exchanges rather than using your desire to feel good to attempt to control someone else. When you attempt to manipulate, exploit, leverage, or force others to do something that will make you feel better, then you attract others who will do the same to you. Attempting to use "guilt trips" is one common means of exploitation. No one can send you on a guilt trip without your willingness to do so. When you honestly communicate by taking responsibility for your feelings, then you open the door to creating a harmonious, loving exchange based on mutual respect and cooperation, and you will attract optimal results.

✕ **Visualize the desired outcome.** Pre-pave the path of your communication by imagining the desired outcome. Your subconscious does not know whether the vibration that you are projecting is because of something you are observing, recalling, currently living, or visualizing. It just responds to your vibration by helping you attract people, situations, and circumstances that are in harmony with your consciousness. But the gloomy reality of any situation does not have to be your truth. Visualize every situation the way you want it to be so that you create a vibrational consciousness that is in harmony with your desire. Then you will attract experiences and people who will be aligned with your desire.

× **Open your communication to the highest good for all.** By doing so, you are allowing yourself to co-create optimally and attract opportunities beyond your current reality. (More about this in Chapter 7.)

× **Communicate from a consciousness of abundance.** You do not have to take a little of what you do not want in an effort to get what you do want. Focus on what you desire, not on the fear of not having what you want. As you maintain this positive focus, you are opening yourself to the highest good for all concerned, and you will access greater abundance.

× **Say yes to what you desire rather than no to what you do not want.** Giving attention to something attracts what you are focusing on into your experience. When you say yes to something, then that something becomes part of your vibration. When you say no to something, however, then that something also becomes part of your vibration. For example, when you say yes to people who treat you respectfully, you attract respect into your experience. However, when you say no to people who treat you disrespectfully, you will attract more disrespect into your experience. The louder you shout NO, the more strength you are giving to what you do not want. Saying no to what you do not want is a forceful demand, which means you are giving your subconscious a clear message to help you attract more of what you are giving attention to. Similarly, saying yes to what you do want is a powerful command to your subconscious to help you attract your desired outcome. The best way to attract more respect is to give attention to what you want rather than align your consciousness with what you do not want.

× **Be aware of the vibrational consciousness you are projecting.** Pay attention to your emotions. Your emotions respond to your thoughts. If you feel positive, then your thoughts are in alignment with your overall desires. If you feel negative, then your thoughts are misaligned with your desires. Negative emotion is a sign that you are giving attention to what you do not want, which means you are in the process of attracting the opposite of what you want. When you feel a negative emotion, it is time for you to ask yourself this question: What new desire does this situation bring forth in me? As soon as you shift your attention to the new desire, you will notice that you will feel better and more in alignment with what you want. For example, when you say, "I do not want to be disrespected," your subconscious mind hears what you are giving attention to, which is disrespect. It does *not* hear, "do not want."

THE BASICS: HOW YOUR VIBRATIONAL LEVEL AFFECTS COMMUNICATION

You project a vibration when you communicate. This vibration is perceived by others. Even when you think no one can tell how you are really feeling, your vibration comes across. We have all felt the vibes when we have walked into a room, even before anyone speaks to us. Higher vibration levels are reflected in effective, compassionate, and assertive communication styles. The lower your vibrational level, the more your communications, both verbal and nonverbal, will be shrouded in a cloud of dense energy. Take the following story, for instance.

Jane is a 32-year-old project manager at a successful marketing firm. Lately it seems as if she is in constant struggle with the other members on her team. Projects are not getting finished on time, and the other members of her team seem to be standing in her way more than working together. Jane is not sure what is going on. Her people used to be an all-star team, but now she is feeling tired, run-down, and worn out by their seeming lack of communication and all-around struggle.

What Jane does not realize is that her team members' lives have changed. Each team member is undergoing personal challenges, and because they do not know how to align their consciousness with their desires, they become stressed. As a result, their stress is impacting their communication and over-all energy. Each person's emotional response to their personal situation impacts their vibrational level, which affects the way they communicates. First there is the thought, next comes an emotional response to that thought, and this emotional re-sponse impacts your vibration. A low vibration often results in miscommunication because we may be seeing things from a pessimistic perspective. Miscommunication creates more nega-tive interactions, unless we consciously and deliberately choose to respond from a sense of well-being rather than fear, anger, or a lack of self-worth. Let us look at Jane's team and find out how their communication is breaking down the team dynamic.

Tom is a 29-year-old graphic designer. He has recently been experiencing some difficulties at home. His girlfriend, whom he has only been seeing a short time, just found out she is pregnant. Tom is (obviously) stressed by this, and his vibrational level is low. When Tom's vibrational level is low, he becomes hostile. He looks for threats around every corner and reacts to others in a defensive manner. He tends to focus on the negative and sees everything as catastrophic. This makes it hard for him to open the lines of communication with his partners. He attracts what he fears the most—the disapproval of others.

Trish, on the other hand, is a cheery, lighthearted, 35-year-old copywriter. Her communication style is open. The thing is, however, Trish doesn't know anything about vibrational levels, and whenever she bumps up against Tom's hostility, her pro-ductivity at work starts to sag. Although she stays strong for a while, eventually she allows herself to become defensive, and after a few attempts at communication, she shuts down and becomes ineffective.

Vikki, 25, is new to the team, and when Jane brought her on to help with the copywriting, she was very impressed with Vikki's go-getter attitude. At first glance, Vikki's energy seems positive because she is always so accommodating and ready to please. However, her people-pleasing attitude actually masks a low vibrational level that shows that Vikki is mired in insecurities. Because her vibrational level is actually low, Vikki runs on one speed—constantly avoiding conflict and trying to keep the peace. She does not move real communication forward, but shuts it down in the name of a calm workplace. Meanwhile, the team can never truly move ahead.

If Jane could see the interactions taking place right in front of her, she might identify the reason for her team's breakdown. Instead, her energy starts to sag as she becomes confused and frustrated. The team cannot co-create if they cannot communicate. But no one sees how their fiery reactions to each other, rather than thoughtful responses, break down their ability to get things done.

What Are the Cues?

The key to effectively co-creating is to raise your own vibrational level. One way you can do this is to remain clear about your intentions and focused on your desires. When we give attention to what we want and release our fears, we create a laser-like energy that speeds manifestation. Like attracts like, and once your vibrational level is high, you will naturally attract people into your life who are in alignment with your intentions. If you bump into people with low vibrational levels, you will be able to maintain your higher level by choosing thoughts that feel good to you. (More about this in Chapter 5.)

First, however, you have to discover your own vibrational level and learn how it is affecting your communication. The easiest way to do this is to look at your communication style.

See if you relate to any of the following styles. If you do, you are going to want to develop new ways of interacting with others to enhance co-creation.

The Aggressive Style: Tom's words and body language are defensive. His aggressive communication style comes across as hostile, as if he is always ready for a fight. Do you relate to any of the following verbal or nonverbal messages?

- ✗ "I'm right and you're wrong, and I'm not giving in!"
- ✗ "I'm not going to let them take advantage of me!"
- ✗ "If I let them have their way, they're going to think they've won and can walk all over me!"

Aggressive communication turns everything into a competition. It spurs all parties on to do anything to win. The underlying belief is that winning earns greater worth.

Whining: Whining is complaining about everything. Whiners see nearly everything as negative. If they cannot find something negative to whine about, they are likely to make something up. Look at the following complaints. How often do you voice them, out loud or silently?

- ✗ "It's so hot outside! It makes it impossible to concentrate!"
- ✗ "They ran out of copier toner at the office supply store. Now I'm going to have to drive all the way across town!"
- ✗ "My boss asked me to stay 30 minutes late today. I'm going to miss my favorite TV show!"

Although these may sound like normal, conversational statements, they are statements that, when made with negative emotion, set you up harmonically to attract more things that displease you rather than attracting things you desire. Whining blocks effective communication by deflecting your attention (and that of people who hear you) from real challenges. It lowers our energy and brings everyone down...except those around you who know how to set their vibrational level on high and in harmony with their desires regardless of the energy others are projecting.

The Silent Treatment: Silence fills the air when an issue arises and people do not speak up. They may feel trapped or fearful that they do not have the right answer. They may feel a lot of things. It's hard to see through their stony exterior. Do any of these statements sound familiar?

- ✗ "Whenever I feel tense, I go blank or just stare out into space."

- ✗ "Whenever I feel conflict going on, all I want is to run away."

- ✗ "When people are upset with each other, I feel frozen. I can't think."

Silence in difficult situations usually leads to greater misunderstanding. Silence may come across as snobbishness or coldness, even though the reality is that the silent person is just scared or nervous. His overwhelming insecurity keeps him from speaking up, which causes him to tolerate the situation rather than find solutions. Tolerating creates negative emotions because people put up with situations when they feel they do not have other options. Feeling that you do not have options is aligned with a scarcity consciousness and inhibits you from being aligned with well-being.

"Agreeing" to solicit the approval of others: Many people try to avoid conflict by always being agreeable. They think that "going with the flow" and always agreeing with everything everyone does or says reduces conflicts in relationships. In reality, they are just pasting a smile on their faces and agreeing. Do you do the following?

- ✗ Nod your head through an entire conversation without truly listening to what the other person is even saying, then telling her you agree.

✗ Say, "No problem," when you are thinking to yourself that this is a ridiculous request and you will never be able to meet the expectation of the person making the request.

✗ Take on extra projects without having a plan for how to manage them.

Although always agreeing may win initial approval, once people discover your lack of authenticity, trust breaks down and communication becomes ineffective. When people are co-creating, everyone needs to give and receive honest feedback. Dishonesty sets us up to attract others who lack integrity into our life.

The One-Up/One-Down Style: One-up/one down is a game in which someone is always trying to prove that he is smarter or better than everyone else. He will always find a way to point out how much more he knows than anyone else in the group. Do any of these statements ring a bell?

✗ Your friend tells you she went to Cancun on vacation and lost all her money. "Well," you reply, "I went on vacation a few years ago and lost all of my money, and then my hotel caught on fire!"

✗ "That will never work. I know it because...."

✗ "You don't know what you're talking about."

✗ "Lemme tell you—this is the way it is...."

✗ "Believe me, I know what I'm talking about!"

The person playing the one-up/one-down game feels driven to prove that she knows best...and is not afraid to tell everyone else how wrong they are. This attitude shuts down communication on many levels and inhibits those involved from having an honest relationship in which everyone is respected for having something valuable to contribute.

Stalling: Do you ever put off doing things that you say are important to you? You make a point of telling people that you will do it, but it never seems to get done. These things might include:

× Waiting until April 14 to complete your taxes.

× Cluttering your house, never putting things away.

× Constantly forgetting to do something you promised to do, such as completing an assignment or trimming the bushes or making that uncomfortable phone call to tell your mother-in-law that you won't be showing up for dinner.

Stalling, or procrastination, is a sign that you don't want to make a decision or take action. It often results in attracting more reasons to feel you can't do whatever it is you are avoiding.

~~~

These are communication styles that inhibit us from attracting desirable outcomes and harmonious relationships. You may not identify with any of these styles, or you may find yourself using more than one style on different occasions. When you are stalling, being aggressive, or saying yes without meaning it, you are blocking effective communication. It is important to begin to communicate from integrity. When you do, you will attract integrity in other people.

BODY LANGUAGE REVEALS OUR HARMONIC VIBRATION

Body language says a lot without words. Remember earlier in the chapter, when I said that people can feel your vibration through the way you communicate, even if you think you are hiding it well? Body language is usually a good indicator of what is going on in your mind and heart. Look at the following list of body language cues and pay attention to how you feel about them:

× Open arms.

× Finger-pointing.

× Looking around.

× Making eye contact.

×   Staring into space.

×   Smiling.

×   Frowning.

×   Leaning forward.

×   Leaning backward.

×   Doodling instead of looking at the other person.

Have you ever been engaged in a conversation with some-one about something serious? Let's say he begins staring into space, looking around, buttoning up his coat in the middle of the conversation, or slumping in his chair. What do you do? You might sit back, look down and away, cross your arms, and slump. His posture shows that he wants to escape the conversation, and your posture shows that you are feeling rejected. Each person is using body language to communicating their true feelings. How you hold yourself sends a message about your vibrational consciousness level. Both you and the other person in this conversation are experiencing low vibrational levels.

When your vibrational level is high, your body language is open. You move freely, your arms hang loosely at your sides or move with conversation, and you lean slightly forward, listening intently to what the other person is saying. You are actively engaged in what is happening in the present. Your body language reflects a genuine interest in co-creating with the other person.

WHAT ARE HIGH-LEVEL HARMONIC VIBRATION STYLES?

The higher your vibration level, the clearer communication becomes. Let's revisit Jane's team. This time, they are all tuned into one another and operating from much higher vibrational levels.

Tom: "Vikki, I didn't get the copy you wrote for that ad I designed. Could you send it to me again?"

Vikki: "I'll be glad to. The attachment must not have gone through."

Tom: "Thanks!"

Originally, when Tom's vibrational level was lower and Vikki was a "yes" person, the conversation might have gone much differently.

Tom: "Vikki, you never sent that copy over. I need that copy! You're making me late finishing this project!"

That would probably be the end of the "conversation." Vikki would nervously scramble to get Tom his copy, perhaps try to lighten his dark mood by commenting on how stupid she was to have forgotten (even if she sent it and it was a simple e-mail mistake). Tom would stomp around the office for the rest of the day.

What did they do in the first example to enhance communication?

When Tom is not being aggressive, he does not use blaming statements. Instead of saying, "You never sent that copy over," he says, "I never received that copy." This simple change of a single word—replacing "you" with "I"—makes a big difference. He is no longer coming at Vikki with an accusation. He is simply stating his reality and checking with Vikki to find out what happened. Now Vikki does not become defensive or scramble to accommodate Tom's hostility. She simply addresses the situation and resends the material. Tom follows up with a thanks for good measure.

Good communication—what you say—is actually the easy part once you have aligned your thoughts, emotions, and beliefs with well-being. The thing that most often trips us up is our insecurity and attention to fear, which colors our perspective and sends us on a mission to either fight our way to the top or slump our way to the bottom rather than working with others as equal co-creators. When your vibrational level is high, you are open-minded and feeling good about yourself. You are aware of options. You feel centered and know that there is more than one solution to any challenging situation. Your communication naturally gravitates toward the effective use of "I" statements. Here are some examples:

× Take responsibility for how you feel, rather than becoming a victim: "I feel hurt when you raise your voice at me. It would feel better to me if we could stay calm when we're having a disagreement."

× Check in with others to determine if you understood them correctly: "I heard you say you feel this way. Am I right?"

× Clarify and ask for information to come to a better understanding: "I'm feeling puzzled by what you just said to me. Please help me to understand why you need space in our relationship."

These statements have one thing in common: They all begin with "I." When you start a statement with "I," it is implied that you are stating your reality. When you begin a statement with "you," it is implied that you are blaming or shaming. "You" statements can be accusatory, and when they are, they signal that you are relinquishing your responsibility for owning your own feelings, thoughts, and deeds. Whenever you say that someone else makes you feel a certain way, you are giving up your power and creating a victim mentality in yourself rather than taking charge of your life. When you relinquish responsibility for how you feel, you attract more and more reasons to feel like a victim.

Insecurity and fear translate into a low vibration. In your struggle to feel in control, you attempt to hide your fear by making someone else wrong. This blocks effective communication. When you feel light-hearted and open and know that ideal solutions are available for every situation, you communicate compassionately, honestly, and harmoniously with others. You use "I" statements because you are comfortable with owning your own reality.

It Begins With Me

The first step to effectively communicating with others is to align your thoughts, beliefs, and emotions with well-being. This is how you raise your vibrational level to be in harmony with the things you desire—prosperity, cooperation, success, understanding, compassion, and so on. When your vibrational level is high, you naturally attract desirable circumstances. When it is low, you attract undesirable situations that leave you feeling powerless. A high vibrational level enables co-creation as a natural, easy process.

Relate to Co-Create

Jamie's boss is making her nervous. He has hardly spoken a word to her for the past several weeks. He has always been very moody and his present silence could be about anything. Let's look at two scenarios and examine how Jamie's feelings about herself impact her ability to communicate and co-create at work. In the first scenario, Jamie is reactive. Her behavior reflects a low vibration:

> To avoid being noticed, Jamie sneaks quietly into work each morning. She is certain her boss is mad at her. Did she make a mistake on a recent report? Did she upset a coworker who has now complained? Did she say something wrong? Did she make some kind of social faux pas? She is constantly wracking her brain to figure out what she has done. Meanwhile, she is having trouble concentrating on getting her work done. She refuses to ask her boss what's going on because she is afraid she might be in trouble, or, worse, get fired.

His silence goes on and on. She continues to have difficulty at the office because she is so afraid.

In the next scenario Jamie responds from a place of self-love and respect, which reflects how she is emotionally in balance, resulting in a high vibrational consciousness.

Jamie makes an appointment to meet with her boss. Once inside his office, she says, "I feel that I can benefit from additional feedback on my work. I'd like to schedule time to discuss my performance so I'll know if I'm meeting your expectations. Then I'll be able to make improvements wherever needed." Now she shows she is not afraid to ask because she's comfortable with both compliments and constructive feedback. She also knows that her ability to co-create at work will be enhanced through open and honest communication with her boss. He tells her that she is doing a fine job, but, if she'd like, they could review her work together each month. She says she'd appreciate that, and now she knows that his silent treatment is not aimed at her at all. It's not about her.

Remember, open and honest communication focuses on finding a solution for the highest good for all concerned. In the first scenario, when Jamie is not feeling good about herself, she goes into avoidance behavior. This inhibits her productivity and creates a lack of clarity between her and her boss. In the second scenario, she opens herself up to honest feedback because she realizes that open communication will help her do a better job for both herself and the company. She feels good about herself and has insight into the fact that co-creating with others, whether at home or at work, involves ongoing communication, which includes giving and receiving honest feedback.

Effective and Ineffective Communication Styles

EFFECTIVE	INEFFECTIVE
Understanding that hostility is directed at what you represent, or at the situation. Usually, it is not you as a person.	Taking hostility personally.
Giving your focused and undivided attention.	Allowing yourself to be distracted by another person, the telephone, etc., unless it is a true emergency.
Recognizing the anger and letting the person know you hear it and can understand it.	Denying the anger or telling the person to calm down.
Listening carefully and fully to what the person says, waiting until he/she is finished.	Continuing to do what you were doing. Brushing people off. Interrupting.
If possible, steering the person to a private area.	Carrying on the conversation in a public place.
Assuming the same position, both of you sitting or both standing.	Having one of you standing, the other sitting.
Keeping your voice calm.	Getting caught up in the emotions and talking in a hostile tone of voice.
Supporting the person without necessarily agreeing.	Arguing or making excuses.

Ultimately, your relationships will be enhanced and co-creation will flow if you take responsibility by using "I" statements and set your intention to communicate:

×   Honestly.

×   Openly.

×   Thoughtfully.

×   Respectfully.

×   Genuinely.

Keep in mind the idea of the highest good for all concerned. When you are focused in the direction of your desires and aligned with well-being, your vibrational consciousness level is high. You feel good about yourself and seek truth and understanding for a joint resolution and co-creation. When you are focused on your fears, you attract one-sided, aggressive communication and engage in right/wrong or black/white thinking. As you raise your vibration, you will be in harmony with and attract others who will take responsibility for themselves. Co-creation and communication will truly flow freely for the best outcomes.

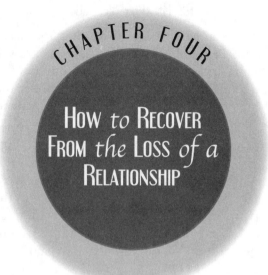

CHAPTER FOUR

How *to* Recover From *the* Loss *of a* Relationship

*In nature, loss is an essential element of creation—
the rose blossoms, the bud is lost; the plant sprouts,
the seed is lost; the day begins, the night is lost. In all
cases, loss sets the stage for further creation...*

—Harold Bloomfield, Melba Colgrove, and
Peter McWilliams

Our relationships orient us in time and space. They are a major part of how we understand who we are. But life does not stay still. Everything grows and changes in time. Sometimes we lose a relationship, and when this happens, we experience disorientation and loss. An important benefit of understanding *The Relationship Code* is learning how to move through loss—and how to live positively in a world of constant change. Whether at home or in the workplace, whether we experience the loss directly or must deal with others in the workplace who experience loss, it is important to have the necessary tools to grow from the experience and move forward in a positive way.

All change can feel like loss if we cling too hard to what we have now. Being alive means learning to grow from every experience, including change, so we can allow ourselves to become something new. It helps to remember that loss is a natural and ongoing part of life. Everyone experiences loss.

It also helps to understand that when we experience a severe loss we often go into shock. When someone tells us, "Snap out of it," this does no good. Recovering from major loss takes time. When we learn the processes of loss and recovery, we can find the emotional codes that give us resiliency in the face of realities that are inevitable. This knowledge helps us build successful lives by teaching us how to transform loss into greater strength and wisdom. We can turn loss into gain.

In our personal lives, family relationships change as we grow. People move to distant locations or experience illness or get married. Sometimes our loved ones die. When a close sibling has a new baby, they no longer have as much time for us. Even though we are happy about the new child, we may experience a sense of lost intimacy. When grown children leave home to go off to college, parents may enjoy more time, but there is still a loss of the familiar situation.

In our professional lives, our work relationships often change. When a favorite boss who has mentored us gets promoted or retires, we experience a loss. Perhaps a coworker decides to resign or take family leave and needs to be home for a long time. Regardless of your feelings toward the person leaving, the whole department has to regroup to deal with this loss, even though it is temporary. Even a very positive change usually involves some feelings of loss. When we have demonstrated great competence, we may be promoted to a challenging new position. Though we are happy about the promotion, we will also experience some sense of loss of the comfort level that comes with familiarity.

We also have relationships with situations, places, and things that become meaningful parts of our identity. When we move to a new home, get a new job, or even buy a new computer system, we often feel a sense of loss of the familiar. We may worry that we will not be as competent in a new environment, and, consciously or unconsciously, we usually grieve the loss of the comfortable place where we used to be.

This chapter explores how to recover from various kinds of relationship losses including the death of someone close to us, the loss of a friendship, changes in a work environment, dealing with other people's losses, and ambiguous losses that leave us uncertain about what we feel. Loss always means a challenge to our identity and our understanding of who we are. Recovery means learning to adapt and let a more colorful identity evolve, take shape, and be integrated into our whole being.

KINDS OF LOSSES

We encounter various kinds of losses, both at home and work, both personally and professionally. Although these kinds of losses have much in common, it is useful to look at them separately. What we see is that losses at home affect performance at work, and vice-versa. The two major spheres of our lives interact. Organizations have found that maintaining a healthy work and home-life balance is beneficial for sustaining effectiveness and a healthy bottom line.

Remember, as you read about different kinds of losses, that we cannot compare one person's loss with another's. We cannot accurately determine the relative severity of one loss versus another. We can only respond to the losses we experience by how we feel. Sometimes what may seem to be a small loss may trigger memories of old losses in which healing was not completed. It is best, therefore, to give ourselves the respect and freedom to heal according to our own inner guidance. In doing so, we also learn to extend others the same respect.

Personal and professional losses can fall into three main categories:

1. Direct loss of a person, situation, or thing.
2. Ambiguous losses (situations of uncertainty).
3. Deceptive losses (that result from upward mobility or upgrades of any kind).

Personal Losses

Some of the types of personal losses we experience in our home life include the following.

Direct losses:

× Death of a loved one or emotionally preparing for the death of a loved one.

× Divorce or loss of love connection.

× Illness or disability.

× Loss of emotional connection within relationships.

× Moving to a new home or location. (This may be a desired or undesired move, such as when the rent or mortgage payment is too high, or following an eviction.)

× Loss or changes in our bodies.

Ambiguous losses (situations of uncertainty):

× Dealing with the what-ifs of on-again, off-again relationships of any kind.

× Awaiting the outcome of missing persons or pets, being uncertain whether they are alive or dead.

× Anticipating results of medical tests (yours or those of someone you care about).

× Dealing with anticipation of chronic health conditions (yours or those of someone you care about, including flare-ups of arthritis, depression, back pain, and so on).

Deceptive losses:

- ✕ Getting married (loss of single lifestyle).
- ✕ Friends getting married (loss of single buddy to hang out with).
- ✕ Buying a new car (loss of old car, your "faithful friend").
- ✕ Upgrades or changes to your home.
- ✕ Receiving a financial windfall (loss of the familiar struggle to make life better).

Losses in our personal lives will affect our working lives, and losses at work will affect our home lives. It is no use pretending otherwise. When a loss is severe, the only solution is to allow ourselves to go through a healing process. If we try to ignore it, the negative impact of loss only gets worse. When we approach loss with compassion and take the time to heal, we can come out of it greatly strengthened and benefit both our families and the organizations we work for with clarity and wisdom.

Professional Losses

Some kinds of professional losses we may experience in our work life are the following.

Direct losses:

- ✕ Loss of a job, project, or promotion.
- ✕ Loss of benefits, including annual raises, healthcare, and vacation perks.
- ✕ Loss of a boss, coworker, or a direct report.
- ✕ Decreased contact with a boss, coworker, or direct report.
- ✕ Loss of a client or a business opportunity.
- ✕ Closure of a department or plant.
- ✕ Loss of your company due to merger or closure.

Ambiguous losses (situations of uncertainty):

- ✗ Dealing with the what-ifs of on-again, off-again work-related decisions.

- ✗ Coping with uncertainty of job status for any reason (yours or that of someone you care about).

- ✗ Dealing with anticipation of retirement.

Deceptive losses:

- ✗ Getting promoted (loss of boss, coworkers, direct reports, and familiar day-to-day tasks).

- ✗ Watching other people at work getting promoted (loss of day-to-day familiar interactions with them, feeling inadequate because you did not get promoted).

- ✗ Accepting a better position in or outside of your current employment.

- ✗ Coping with upgrades or changes to your office, such as moving from a cubicle to an office with a window, or changes to your office setting, such as getting new computers, software, and so on (loss of familiarity).

- ✗ Receiving a financial windfall (loss of the familiar struggle to make life better).

Losses are a normal part of work life, right alongside gains. We become used to the rough-and-tumble of work and build up habits of denying loss that can become like calluses on our skin. Whereas being calloused may serve us in the day-to-day routine, it can become a barrier when we need to deal with more severe losses and their emotional impact because it can greatly diminish our ability to perform when we don't know how to deal with great emotional pain.

We live in an environment of intense change. To be a successful person, to build successful relationships, and to sustain successful organizations, we need to understand the processes of loss. Learning how to recover from the losses that everyone experiences is as important to building sustainable organizations as having a disaster recovery plan to protect the organization's data. Successfully managing relationship loss is a critical element of transition management and protection of human capital. Without it, organizations fall apart.

Ambiguous Losses

All change has an element of uncertainty—life is not predictable. Sometimes we experience confusing situations in which we don't know what will happen or whether the situation is a loss or a gain. Often, it may be both. Will a merger bring us a promotion or cost us our job? Will a separation result in a renewed marriage or a divorce? Will a missing friend, family member, coworker, or pet be found alive or dead? Will our medical test results show a fatal diagnosis? These are all examples of ambiguous situations that have a component of loss. Even if they turn out for the good, we go through a period of contemplating and feeling loss. Thus, this aspect of loss is always near at hand. It helps to make friends with the truth of ambiguity. Sometimes loss can help us learn to be more flexible and intuitive about our whole approach to life.

Ambiguous losses are real, of course, and need to be acknowledged and addressed so that we do not allow our emotions to get the best of us, which can easily lead to self-sabotage. I once worked with a man, Art, who shared a bit of his personal past with me as we discussed the much-anticipated acquisition of the company where we worked. Art's response to the fear running rampant in our organization was to hold steady and sit tight while he gathered more information from the company executives. His calmness was contrary to the reaction of nearly everyone else, individuals who were jumping ship early to avoid the fear that they might lose their jobs later on. Art was one of the few people who did not react negatively to the anticipated buyout, which was at least a year away. When I asked him how he could remain so calm when others were so fearful, he shared a personal story that he felt had taught him valuable lessons.

Art told me that, years ago, Sandy, his first wife, had vehemently protested that being married was not the most important part of her life. There were other things in her life that were equally important to her. She wanted to consider having a career and perhaps explore some hobbies. He was so threatened by this intense discussion of her dissatisfaction with this stage of her life, coupled with her strong desire to make a career the focal point of her existence, that he reacted out of fear. In anticipation of being left alone, he demanded they get divorced. He confided to me that he did not want to end the marriage, as she was the love of his life. The realization of her unhappiness caused him to anticipate her leaving him, and this was more than he could bear. For him, making a decision to leave the marriage was less painful than dealing with the ambiguity of the situation. It was his way of taking control of his life and ensuring he was not left alone. Soon after their separation, he started dating others. He remarried immediately after his divorce was finalized. Art shared with me that his second wife, Jan, was a friend and devoted companion, but his feelings for her did not match the love and passion he still felt for Sandy. Years later, after the ambiguity of the situation had passed, he realized that Sandy never intended to leave him. He was devastated to realize that he had reacted in such haste, and, in his words, "made a mess of things."

What we can learn from Art's story is that in ambiguous situations we need to respond rather than react, gather information by listening more and talking less, and seek the wise counsel of others (friends and professionals) who are not entrenched in our situation. It is best to slow down and check in with others rather than make assumptions, which almost always attract our worst fears.

Deceptive Losses

It often comes as a surprise that even a positive change can feel like a loss. For example, when you successfully complete a major project, you may feel the loss of a clear long-term goal. You may miss the invigorating teamwork of a group of people working hard together to achieve something meaningful. People often feel a kind of post-partum depression after a great success. You may wonder what you will do for an encore. Success sometimes brings the end of a great effort that gave meaning to your life. You may feel all the symptoms of loss because it is a kind of loss and is best treated as such.

STAGES OF RECOVERY

With minor losses, we may move through the stages of recovery in minutes, whereas major losses may take years to fully recover from. But keep in mind the fact that every recovery comprises four stages. These stages apply to all kinds of losses, great or small, in personal life and in professional life.

1. Survival.
2. Healing.
3. Growth.
4. Thriving.

If we get stuck somewhere in the process, or if we try to rush our recovery faster than our inner process requires, we will have incomplete recovery. The next time we experience loss, we may have to recover from earlier unresolved losses as well.

Nothing can bring you peace but yourself.
—Ralph Waldo Emerson

Survival

You have survived. You will continue to survive.

The first normal reactions to loss are denial and numbness. Your mind rejects the whole idea that the loss has happened.

You feel stunned every time you remember the loss, and then you forget it again. This is part of our natural protective mechanism against intense pain. By denying the loss, we are cushioned in numbness so that we can gradually come to terms with the pain. A little denial is not a bad thing. Like a blister on a burn, it protects us while we get used to the shock.

As we begin to come out of the fog of initial shock, however, we begin to feel some of the natural emotions that arise in response to the loss. We feel fear, anger, and sadness. As you go through the recovery process, you may feel a wide range of emotions, some of which may seem strange to you. It is important to allow every feeling to flow through you without judging it and without taking it out on yourself or others.

In the beginning, the main thing is to allow yourself to feel. Just be with your feelings. No matter what you feel, you will get better. The survival and healing process does have an end.

If you feel depressed or suicidal or think that you need help, get it without delay. Call a professional licensed therapist or a suicide hotline immediately. It is important that you receive professional help to support you in the healing process.

As you begin to acknowledge the loss, you may go back and forth between fear and numbness for a while. It is okay to feel what you feel—and it is also okay not to feel. Your system knows what it needs for its healing. It is very smart that way, and it will guide you through your recovery.

When we have begun to accept that the loss has happened, we usually feel anger. It is okay to feel anger toward whomever you feel angry toward. But it is not okay to act on that anger by blaming yourself or others or by being abusive. Moving through loss is about feeling, not about acting out. Feeling anger does not require action; you can just sit with it and let it flow through you until, in its own time, it may transform into strength.

I once hired a manager who initially seemed excellent in dealing with the staff who reported to him. Months later, however, I started hearing complaints about him from the staff. I would walk by his office and hear him yelling at the therapists he supervised. When I discussed this with him, he replied that he was going through a divorce. I clearly saw that he was experiencing a lot of pent-up anger. Although his inappropriate behavior at work may have stemmed from his loss at home, regardless of the source, he needed to acknowledge his feelings without taking them out on others. I referred him to the employee assistance program to give him an emotional outlet to address his personal concerns. This proved helpful to both him and the organization, as he was able to move through his loss and regain the trust and respect of his staff. It is quite natural to feel hurt. You can allow yourself to sit with the hurt. You may also feel deep grief, sorrow, exhaustion, confusion, melancholy, sadness, giddiness, silliness, relief, guilt, self-hatred, envy, disgust, rage, and any other feeling you can name. You may feel like a failure. You may feel lost, beaten, uncertain, and overwhelmed. All of these feelings are part of the healing process. It is okay to feel contradictory feelings too. There are no forbidden feelings.

You are alive. You have survived. Even if you feel dead inside, you will come back to life.

Every now and then, between bouts of feeling whatever comes, it is good to remind yourself that you are a good and worthwhile person. Try to avoid punishing yourself by imagining that you could have done something to avoid the loss. This is just a useless self-criticism. Your opportunity in this stage is simply to come to terms with the loss and move toward healing.

Healing

Indicators that you have moved from survival to healing include:

×　You are more aware of your emotions.

×　You respond to others rather than react to them.

×　Periodically, you smile.

As the initial denial and numbness wear off, you may feel more pain, but feeling anything is a sign of life returning. You are beginning the healing stage.

You have felt many emotions and now you are beginning to look into them a little more deeply. By taking the time to process emotions, you can gain new understanding and eventually let them go. But don't hurry them. Let your feelings teach you what they mean. Honor them, for they are the truth of what you are feeling now. As you heal, you will come to realize that they are not your permanent identity, but for now, your feelings need to be honored. If you do not allow them to process, they will stay buried within you and cause you trouble until you let them have their say.

Loss disrupts our sense of identity. We may have defined ourselves by a job or a marriage that is no more, and now we may be wondering who we are. If the relationship is gone, you ask yourself, who am I? The new reality may seem very strange. However, our true identity is not limited by any relationship or place or position. From infancy to adulthood, human beings grow and change. We build new identities as we grow, and you will discover a new and greater identity by healing and recovering from your loss.

Here are nine ways to move through loss, heal, and recover:

1. Grieving and being with your feelings.
2. Taking care of yourself (with rest, good nutrition, and peace).
3. Pampering yourself and indulging in healthy pleasures.
4. Having a regular routine that is not overly stressful.
5. Keeping a dream journal or a notebook to record your feelings and intentions.

6. Staying connected to people who are uplifting.
7. Forgiving yourself and others.
8. Anticipating good things to look forward to.
9. Visualizing a positive future.

Grieving usually includes a lot of different emotions and follows a logic that is not always obvious to our conscious mind. How can we feel terrible sorrow and gladness at the same time? How can we suddenly laugh in the middle of tears? How can we feel guilty that the loss was "all our fault" and at the same time feel blame and rage toward another person we are certain has been the cause of our loss? Well...we just can. Grieving follows its own mysterious path, and its logic is hidden in the inner wisdom each of us has.

It is okay to feel remorse for things we said and did. You can allow feelings of guilt and shame to flow through you. But it is not healthy to dwell on self-punishing emotions. Grieving is about processing and understanding and healing. It is not about attacking yourself and making the loss worse. This is an important time to be aware of self-deprecation and to consciously shift to being compassionate toward yourself.

When you are healing from a major loss, you also benefit from taking a nap. Lots of rest and sleep are very helpful to your healing process. You will probably know when it is time to get up and get moving again. Even after your initial steps in the healing stage, you may need extra sleep from time to time. This is good medicine for the body and the soul. It can also be restful to have a stable day-to-day routine that keeps you occupied and lightly productive.

Your dreams are often a place where healing emotions get worked out. You may want to keep a dream journal beside your bed and write down your dreams when you wake up. They may give you insights into feelings you are processing. The idea is to let the feelings flow through, and not to cling to them or to push them away, but just to allow them to move and release.

Even if you need to be alone some of the time, it is best not to isolate yourself. Stay connected to people you trust. Talk to intimate friends or professional counselors about what you are going through and allow them to support you emotionally. Laughter is a wonderful healer.

If you let all the feelings that arise flow through you, they will eventually clear. It is like water flowing through a dirty pipe—at first, what comes out is muddy and dark, but if the water keeps flowing, the mud is gradually flushed out and the water becomes clearer. When you are ready—and not before you feel ready—you can begin to forgive all the other people involved in the loss. Forgive yourself too.

Forgiveness is the only way to finally let go of the hurt so you can move on. Though forgiving may benefit others, its primary beneficiary is you. By forgiving, you allow yourself to release the past and flush away all the negative feelings. Until you give yourself this gift, you will remain to some degree stuck in the past that you are holding. Choose to let go.

Anticipate good things to come. It is important to allow yourself a sufficient period of mourning for your loss, but it is also important to remember that it will pass. Grieving is only a passage, not your whole life. Look forward toward a positive outcome. You may find it helpful to write in your notebook and set some new goals for your life.

Always write in positive language: Write what you do want rather than what you do not want. If what comes first is about what you *don't* want, you can rephrase it to say that you *do* want the opposite, and then spell it out. You may have a strong feeling that you don't want to have people in your life who don't appreciate you. It is best to write the positive: *I want people in my life who appreciate me.* We attract whatever we focus on, so focus on what you truly want and let your good feelings connect with that outcome.

Visualize a positive future. Think about what you want your new life to be like and hold an image of that good future in your mind. Set a strong intention that you will be guided toward your highest good and that all your intentions will be aligned with the best interests of all concerned. When you ask for positive guidance, you will get an outcome even better than you imagined.

Tips for Day-to-Day Living While Moving Through a Significant Loss

- ✗ Set reasonable goals for yourself.
- ✗ Set priorities; do what you can.
- ✗ Break large tasks into small ones.
- ✗ Take everything at your own pace.
- ✗ Stay connected with others.
- ✗ Take walks and exercise if this is acceptable to your physician.
- ✗ Shift from pessimistic thinking to hopeful thoughts.

Growth

Sometimes it may seem like magic or alchemy when healing starts to become growth. You may find yourself surprised to discover that the new identity that is forming in you is stronger than the old identity. Recovering from a loss has given you many gifts, and you are more whole and more capable of dealing with your human emotions now than you were before.

You will almost certainly have more compassion for others who are suffering a loss. The recovery process often moves back and forth between stages for a while. Remember to also have compassion for yourself when you experience an occasional setback.

Aspects of the growth stage include the following:

- ✗ You are building strength.
- ✗ You are feeling compassion for yourself rather than feeling victimized.

×   You are learning and willing to let go.

×   You are learning and willing to forgive.

×   You are appreciating what you have gained.

×   You are honoring your courage.

×   You are embracing relationships, both old and new.

×   You are ready to begin your new life.

As you find yourself feeling your new strength, try new things. Just go gently at first. Do it, but don't overdo it. Keep doing the things that make you feel stronger and more alive.

Forgive any person you felt wronged by, and forgive yourself for judging them. It was natural at the time, but now feeling victimized is a burden you can drop. Forgive yourself for any failings you thought may have contributed to the loss. Nobody is perfect. Whatever you may have done or said, or failed to do or say, is past. No good comes from beating yourself up about it. Forgive yourself for judging yourself. One good lesson that can come from recovery is that being harsh with yourself benefits no one. Being compassionate with yourself often leads to greater compassion for others. Forgive and be free.

Appreciate all the good you gained from the relationship you had. It must have given you a great deal or you would not have missed it so much. By appreciating what you gained, you can keep the good with you, even as you let go of the bad.

Honor yourself for having the courage to survive the loss, heal, and grow. Much wisdom, compassion, and strength comes from having the courage to go through every stage of the recovery process. You are a richer person as a result of all you have learned. Honor your courage.

Go forward and grow into your new life. Reach out and meet new people and new situations. Don't be afraid to trust again. Yes, you have come through a loss, but you have re-covered. That's life. It has its ups and downs—and then its ups again. Embrace the creative flow of new relationships and the tested endurance of old ones. Thank the people who have helped you to recover. Celebrate with them.

Thriving

One thing loss and recovery can teach you is that you are more resilient than you may have thought. Now that you know you can recover, why settle for just healing and growth? Why not create a life that is even better than before? Why not *thrive*?

Aspects of transformation in the thriving stage include:

× Regaining your passion.

× Refocusing on a new purpose.

× Engaging in life.

× Empowering yourself and others.

× Recognizing that loss and recovery have made you richer, wiser, and stronger.

When you recognize that loss and recovery have given you new gifts, you are taking a step toward empowering yourself. By engaging in your life with renewed energy, you discover ways you can use your gifts to empower others. This can guide you to find new purpose and reawaken your passion for life.

FORGIVENESS

In my work with individuals, couples, and organizations—and, of course, in my own self-exploration—I have seen many circumstances in which forgiveness was called for in order to move forward in a positive direction. Forgiveness is called for when we have judged ourselves, others, or situations. Judgment always creates a consciousness within us of being a victim. It holds us back from taking charge of our lives and positions us to attract more reasons to feel victimized. Remember that the subconscious mind works on our behalf to help us attract and create circumstances that foster our beliefs about ourselves and others. By being willing to forgive, you are giving yourself the gift of taking charge of your life in a positive direction.

Even the most positive change requires letting go of something
familiar and accepting something new in its place.
          —Linda Fisher and Rose Kennedy

PROCESSING LOSS IN ORGANIZATIONAL TRANSITIONS

Because of today's fast pace and high rate of change, many organizations must confront challenges arising from processing feelings of loss during transitions. Loss is an essential aspect of change.

I was called into an organization to do its annual culture analysis shortly after it had begun a restructuring. In the process, I discovered that the company was being negatively affected by projects being held in limbo because of the loss of some managerial staff.

As I learned that the emotional issues associated with the restructuring were not being acknowledged and addressed, I gave the following recommendations:

× Hold focused meetings with certain departments to address loss and coach them in the Harmonic Matching Process to move them forward more expeditiously.

× Give those most affected a chance to talk through and create a personal action plan to deal with their feelings.

× In some cases, provide executive coaching for leaders to guide them how to move their employees through the change process in a better way.

× Provide team-building interventions for teams that are floundering.

The company implemented these suggestions, and six months later, I did a follow-up culture analysis review that included employee surveys and management interviews. These showed positive results. Staff retention was up; employee morale had improved because people felt that the leaders cared about them, which is a critical component of leadership; several critical projects were back on track; and organizational productivity was up.

In today's climate of intense change, addressing the emotional component of loss associated with change can make an enormous difference for organizations. Specific leadership actions are called for to appropriately manage transition in an organization. Toward the end of this chapter, I give at-a-glance tables that specify employee emotions and responses during various stages of transition, along with the corresponding leadership actions required to successfully guide employees through various stages of transformation. These tables also describe the price individuals and organizations can pay when the recovery process is not implemented.

Recovery Toolbox: Uplifters

This toolbox summarizes some of the "uplifters" that empower you to move through your recovery process toward a thriving new life filled with beautiful relationships and creative opportunities.

× **Accept** your feelings.

× **Understand the loss** and that change is an inevitable part of life.

× **Appreciate** all the good times you had in the past.

× **Feel gratitude** for what you have learned and gained.

× **Forgive** and let go. Release all negativity and become free.

× **Realize** that the best of the past remains within you as gifts.

× **Honor** the lost relationship by moving on with your life.

×   **Intend** positive outcomes for all stages of your recovery.

×   **Envision** a thriving future of positive relationships.

×   **Finish old business** by communicating within yourself. Consider writing a letter to anyone you cannot communicate with directly. Do not, however, mail the letter. Keep it in your journal.

When you cannot resolve old business with someone because they are gone or because communication has broken down, you can imagine the other person and communicate with them in your mind. You can also write them a letter, which you hold on to. This has proven to be a time-honored and effective way of completing old issues so that they do not weigh down your recovery process. Many people believe that this inner communication can be subtly received by others who are far away. The main point, however, is that you can use this method to let go and free yourself from old tangles.

Checklist for Helping Others Deal With Loss

1. Communicate.

    a. Acknowledge the situation.

    b. Genuinely express concern.

    c. Be an empathetic listener.

    d. Be compassionate and supportive.

    e. Completely accept the person's feelings.

    f. Stay clear of *should*, *must*, and *ought* statements, which create judgment and limit the person's options.

    g. Use words/statements such as *could*, *might consider*, *perhaps*, and *think about*, which show respect and create options without telling a person what to do.

   h. Allow short and long periods of silence during conversation.

   i. Check in with the person and ask what would be helpful to her.

2. Provide support.

   a. Ask what would be helpful to him and offer your support accordingly.

   b. Be aware that what she needs today may be different tomorrow or next week.

   c. Stay clear of making assumptions.

3. Pay attention to the warning signs of depression. Depression is a serious medical illness that impacts how you think, feel, and behave. Although they may look the same, grief and depression are different. Symptoms of depression may include:

   a. Deep sadness.

   b. Significant loss of pleasure in activities once enjoyed.

   c. Changes in appetite resulting in weight losses or gains unrelated to dieting.

   d. Insomnia or sleeping significantly more than usual.

   e. Increased fatigue.

   f. Irritability or restlessness.

   g. Feelings of guilt, shame, or worthlessness.

   h. Difficulty concentrating or making decisions.

   i. Thoughts of death, suicide gestures or attempts.

(Symptoms of depression derived from the American Psychiatric Association (APA). © 2010 American Psychiatric Association, the National Institute of Mental Health (*www.nimh.nih.gov*), and the National Mental Health Association (*www.nmha.org*).)

You can be depressed and not experience every symptom. Some people experience only a few symptoms, whereas others experience many. The severity of symptoms varies through time and from person to person. Depression is very treatable. If someone you know is experiencing these symptoms, immediately refer them to a licensed therapist or medical physician.

SUMMARY

The tables on the following pages provide you with an at-a-glance summary of the four stages of loss, appropriate actions for leaders in organizations, the positive outcomes when loss is recognized and dealt with correctly during each stage, and the unnecessary challenges that occur when an organization does not take appropriate action. Study and use these tables to guide yourself and others through organizational change as well as personal loss.

Stage 1: Survival

One day at a time.

Emotions & Responses	Leadership Actions for Organizations	Positive Outcomes for Individuals & Organizations
Emotions: Denial Shock Numbness Fear Anger Responses: Confusion Disengagement Disincentive	Listen carefully. Acknowledge loss associated with change. Maintain communication. Offer support and address emotions. Adjust and stabilize day-to-day routine. Tell the truth.	Allows healing and recovery to occur. Change and loss are better understood. Employees believe leaders care. Organization grows closer in dealing with loss rather than fragmenting.

Price organization can pay if loss is not dealt with appropriately:

Disintegration and lack of clarity about goals.

Decrease in morale, increased absenteeism, higher turnover.

Loss of productivity and decreased sustainability.

Price individual can pay at home and at work:

Sense of failure and decreased functionality.

Reduced creativity, lack of courage, and lost sense of purpose.

Stage 2: Healing

Being okay with your feelings.

Emotions & Responses	Leadership Actions for Organizations	Positive Outcomes for Individuals & Organizations
Emotions: Sadness Ambivalence Responses: Self-Care Connection Processing Forgiveness Anticipation Visualization	Acknowledge loss. Support recovery. Encourage connection. Guide processing. Seek and stimulate forgiveness. Inspire positive future focus. Build credibility.	Successful recovery. Re-energized teams. Group learning. Process negative feelings to start with clean slate. Shared effort leading to organizational cohesion.

Price organization can pay if loss is not dealt with appropriately:

Incomplete healing leaving unresolved negative feelings.

Organizational fragmentation and reduced sustainability.

Reduced productivity and effectiveness.

Price individual can pay at home and at work:

Sense that organization does not care, and loss of drive.

Feelings of failure leading to loss of connection with family.

Stage 3: Growth

Compassion: being willing to stop criticizing
yourself or others.

Emotions & Responses	Leadership Actions for Organizations	Positive Outcomes for Individuals & Organizations
Emotions: Less anxiety Acceptance Hope Responses: Renewal Negotiation Experimenting Forming new relationships	Encourage creative solution-building. Celebrate renewal. Support open dialogue and participation. Set new goals, processes, and policies. Provide training. Model integrity.	Stable individuals. Revitalized organizations. Elevated morale. Increased effectiveness and productivity. Embrace change. Courage to move forward.

Price organization can pay if loss is not dealt with appropriately:

Unrealistic goals and budgets; false starts and stagnation.

Loss of focus; things falling through the cracks.

Price individual can pay at home and at work:

Inability to forgive and let go.

Lack of appreciation for gains.

Resistance to change

Resistance to growth.

Stage 4: Thriving

Recognizing and appreciating gifts stemming from your loss.

Emotions & Responses	Leadership Actions for Organizations	Positive Outcomes for Individuals & Organizations
Emotions: Empowerment Engagement Passion Purpose Responses: Adaptive Creativity Enhanced Productivity	Reward and empower. Invite engagement. Inject enthusiasm and nourish passionate team participation. Integrate and clarify new purpose. Encourage and focus team creativity and vision.	Flexible and adaptive competitive advantage. Enthusiastic morale. Super performance and creativity. Focused and sustainable evolving vision. Employee retention.

Price organization can pay if loss is not dealt with appropriately:

Complacency and settling for "good enough."

Inattention to rapidly evolving environment; unready for next change.

Over-cautiousness stifles creativity and open participative dialogue.

Price individual can pay at home and at work:

> Risk aversion stifles willingness to try new things.
>
> Preferring momentary comfort to creative exploration and adventure.
>
> Inhibition of courage to dream and believe in big visions.

This is a time of rapid change in which everyone experiences some degree of loss. By understanding the aspects of loss described here and the Harmonic Matching Process described in Part II of this book, you will navigate life more successfully.

PART II
Harmonic Matching: Four Steps to Fulfill Relationship Intentions

You can transform your emotions so that positive intention takes its rightful place as the leader of your life and attracts successful relationships and opportunities. The Relationship Code is the four-step Harmonic Matching Process, which shows how you can learn to create a life in which you take control of your destiny.

THE FOUR STEPS: OVERVIEW OF THE HARMONIC MATCHING PROCESS

The better you understand the Harmonic Matching Process, the more effectively you will be able to create desirable outcomes. This process is the essence of The Relationship Code that frees you from the tyranny of unconscious negative beliefs and gives you the keys to successful relationships and opportunities. There are four steps to attracting positive relationships and opportunities at work and at home. (Refer to Figure 5-1, Harmonic Matching Process.)

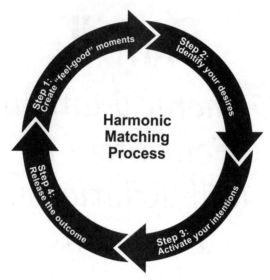

Figure 5-1
Harmonic Matching Process

1. Create feel-good moments.
2. Identify your desires.
3. Activate your intentions.
4. Release the outcome.

The first step energizes your emotional resources and elevates your feelings to the highest positive states. This fills your heart and mind with the juice to manifest your desires.

The second step identifies your desires and clarifies them in thought as well as defined relationship goals. It defines the target you intend to reach.

The third step activates your intentions by integrating them with the positive energy of your desires. This is like drawing back the bow and aiming at the target.

The fourth step allows you to release your intention in a relaxed and focused way. It guides you to align yourself with faith to create a beneficial outcome. When the arrow flies free, it is no longer in your control; you must let go and trust that your highest good will come to you.

CHAPTER FIVE

STEP ONE: Create Feel-Good Moments

When dealing with people, remember you are not dealing with creatures of logic, but creatures of emotion.
—Dale Carnegie

FOCUS ON GOOD MEMORIES

You can use your conscious mind to intentionally focus on the most positive memories in your life. This conscious act draws up the emotional energy of your most wonderful experiences to fill up a reservoir of good feelings that lift your mental and emotional state. We feel better when we think about the times we have been happiest, the times we had our best successes, and the times we enjoyed the most creative relationships.

Focusing on good memories is the most valuable use of your time. Every successful person intuitively knows this powerful practice. You are charging your emotional batteries and building up your emotional muscles to create the life you desire. When you build up these resources, you will have them available when you need them to sustain a positive orientation to deal with a challenging situation at home or at work. Everyone possesses a storehouse of special memories charged with good feelings. Rummage around in your memories and bring these treasures to the top of your mind, where you can recall them in greater detail and cherish them. They are the golden ore that you can use to build new successes. This is something you can do when waiting in line at the grocery store, while riding on a train, or even before a meeting that fills you with anxiety.

What are your best memories? Do you remember a beautiful day when you were having fun? Can you recall a time when you achieved something special? How about the pride you felt? What about the blissful feeling that spread over you when you were kissed by someone special? Will you ever forget how happy you felt when you won that special dream job? Or the feeling of triumph and happiness you felt on graduation day?

Each of us has our own unique moments. You might remember the day you were alone in a beautiful natural environment or the evening when you were celebrating with friends in a big city. There are no universal rules for what feels good. The only thing that matters is that your memories *make you feel good*. It benefits you to keep these precious memories and the feelings they evoke close to the top of your mind.

One of the wonderful things about being human is that we can revisit our special moments whenever we wish. When we do so, they become part of our present experience. The pleasure we feel as we immerse ourselves in these experiences is something we feel now—in the present moment. These are real feelings. Each time we revisit them, they become stronger. In addition to making us feel good, happy memories also have the power to elevate our energy levels, increase our self-esteem, and even boost our immune systems!

Pick one memory that feels particularly pleasurable to you and dive into it right now. Go to your moment of greatest pleasure. What does it feel like? What do you most like about it? What are you seeing? What does the setting look like? What do you hear? Do any special words come into your thoughts? What do you feel? Maybe you can remember how the sun and the breeze felt on your skin. Can you remember what you were wearing? What do you smell? Was there a special fragrance in the air? What do you taste? It doesn't matter what the memory brings as long as it makes you feel good. You might have a pleasurable memory of the smell of your grandfather's after-shave, for example, and the thought of this fragrance brings you back to the sweet memory of the day you went hiking with him.

To make the memory as vivid as possible, try to retrieve as many sensory cues and feeling states as possible. Try to evoke all five physical senses—sight, hearing, smell, taste, and touch. These memories build up your store of positive feelings that are sometimes called "resource states." Each resource state we develop gives us strength to create new successes and new feel-good moments. As you explore your memories, collect moments for as many positive emotions as possible, times when you felt successful, peaceful, joyous, loved, smart, proud, powerful, skillful, happy, or contented. Each emotion enriches your store of emotional energy and elevates your state. Smile and laugh aloud as you think of good times.

FEEL GOOD ABOUT YOURSELF

The more you radiate positive thoughts and feelings, the more you attract those energies into your life. When you are sending out negative thoughts, it is very difficult to attract the relationships you really desire. The easiest way to let old negative emotions drift away from you is to fill your thoughts and feelings with positive emotions that push them out.

What do you love? Think about that. Just enjoy allowing yourself to feel the pleasure of thinking about what you love. Select three activities that you enjoy; whatever makes you feel good.

What are you good at? It doesn't matter what you choose; whatever feels appealing to you. Think about doing those things. Notice how your mood is getting brighter? Choose one activity or memory and focus on how you felt at the moment it was happening. Allow yourself to enjoy the glow. Breathe deep and relax into the feeling.

Close your eyes and imagine that you are on your way to a favorite place of your choosing, a place where you can feel a deep sense of inner peace. For example, you might see yourself on a beautiful beach on a day when the temperature is just right for you. You feel the wind in your hair, smell the salt of the ocean, hear the lapping of the waves, and feel the warmth of the sun. You can travel anywhere in your mind and you can rearrange the setting to suit what you most enjoy.

Use your imagination. You can intentionally use it to lift your mood and elevate your self-esteem. You can do this anytime, anywhere. When you set the positive intention to feel good about yourself, you are doing one of the most valuable things you can do for yourself...and for everyone around you as well. Good feelings attract good feelings. Don't be surprised if people smile at you on the street after you have been exploring positive memories and feelings. It's natural.

What an amazing discovery this is, that you can *choose* to direct your mind toward positive experiences that create positive emotions, and that this attracts positive relationships and opportunities into your life. For example, on your way to work you might focus on a memory of a day when you achieved a notable success, and how good you felt about it. When you get to your workplace, your whole being will radiate positive energy that will attract a positive response from your boss and coworkers, resulting in a more productive day. Years ago, I was commuting to work and thinking about how unappreciated I felt by the individuals in the organization. Knowing that by giving attention to this situation I was setting myself up to attract other people in my life who did not appreciate me, I deliberately changed my mind and chose to focus on all the times that others demonstrated appreciation for the extra things I did for them. Several hours later, when I arrived at my destination, I was greeted by the CEO, who made a point of telling me how much she appreciated the extra effort I had provided on a specific project. A few minutes later, one of my employees stopped me in the hall and expressed gratitude for the mentoring I had offered him. Taking the time to focus on what I desired rather than what was irritating to me created a feel-good moment, which inspired me to go the extra mile for my employer.

THE LAW OF ATTRACTION: LIKE ATTRACTS LIKE

The Law of Attraction is in alignment with what we know about the subconscious. It is the basis for how resources and opportunities flow to us and from us. It impacts our relationships as well, in that we attract individuals into our experience who affirm what we believe about ourselves, about others, and about life situations and circumstances. The Law of Attraction can be defined as follows: What we believe and what we focus on becomes our experience. In essence, the self-fulfilling prophecy is a real phenomenon that, if paid attention to, can change our lives for the better. The best motivational and sales materials ever written, from *How to Win Friends and Influence People* and *Think and Grow Rich* to *How to Master the Art of Selling* and *The One-Minute Manager*, all use the universal and timeless principles of the Law of Attraction for greater success and well-being.

We attract what we give attention to or what we focus on. If we focus our thoughts on our true desires, we can attract them. However, if we focus on not having what we want, we will create obstructions that repel our desires. Beliefs are patterns of thought. We attract experiences that are in alignment with our beliefs. For example, if we desire a good job that fulfills us and pays us well, but we believe we are unworthy or have little to offer a potential employer, then a satisfying job will not be forthcoming. The subconscious is just doing its job and helping us attract what we believe we will get.

Whatever we believe about ourselves will be affirmed through the Law of Attraction. Thus, individuals who attract jobs that are not satisfying for them are affirming over and over again their greatest beliefs about themselves—that they are not worthy of fulfilling work and appropriate rewards.

Like the Law of Gravity, the Law of Attraction is an invisible force. Though we cannot see gravity, we can see the results of it. Neither can we see the Law of Attraction, but we can see the results of it as we correlate our thoughts, beliefs, and emotions with the experiences we are creating.

EMOTIONAL TRANSFORMATION

Emotions create waves of energy that move our thoughts and desires throughout space and time. The stronger the emotion, the more powerful the movement, attracting whatever we are giving our attention to in that moment. The stronger the emotion—positive or negative—the more quickly our thoughts create our experiences.

Our thoughts can be focused in one of two directions: either our intention to have something we desire, or our fear of not having it. It is difficult to monitor our thoughts because they come so quickly into our minds. It is much easier to pay attention to our emotions. Our emotions provide guidance to us with regard to the direction of our thoughts. When our emotions are positive, our thoughts are in alignment with our desires. When our emotions are negative, our thoughts are not in alignment with our desires. Whatever we focus our thoughts on is what we attract into our experience.

An Example of Positive Realignment

At one point in my executive career, I had a vacancy in my department for an assistant director position. I decided to open it to people outside the department to interview for the position rather than limit myself to my internal group. Hilary, a supervisor on my staff, was upset that she had not been solicited to apply for the position. She approached me and told me she was distraught by this and asked why she had not been automatically promoted into that role.

I replied that what I was looking for did not seem to be a match to her skill sets. At that point she had a choice: She could have gotten angry and been defensive, she might have gone to HR and filed a complaint or even quit the department in her anger. Instead, she went home and thought about it. That evening, Hilary spoke to a good friend and reviewed her options. As a result, she was able to make a positive shift in her emotions. She drafted a document saying how she could meet the criteria I had outlined for that role, including what she would do to learn skills in the areas she needed to strengthen.

It turns out Hilary was the best person for the job. Because she chose to focus on her desire instead of her fear, Hilary created a feel-good moment. She felt good about herself, and, as a result, she was able to be inspired to provide me with what I needed to feel good about her in that role. The outcome was that she was with me for many years and did a fabulous job.

To help you get to know the flow of your emotions and practice focusing them in positive directions, study the following Table of Emotional Transformations. This shows the harmonic scale of emotions and the transformation from negative to positive for each. If you see that you are focusing on a negative you do not want, you can choose to refocus on a positive you do want and train yourself to transform your emotions.

Notice that emotion words are just descriptors that can help you explore the full richness of your emotional life. Also, transformations are not always directly to the immediate opposite. Emotions flow constantly from one state to another. You might experience a journey from feeling rejected to angry to hurt to forgiving to peacefulness to self-appreciation. The point of the table is to give you a few terms to help you identify feelings. You can add your own words and learn by observing how your feelings evolve. You can be truthful to your feelings in the present moment, then move on to more positive states by shifting your focus. Transformation is about positive creativity, not about denial.

Table of Emotional Transformations

Negative Emotions	Positive Emotions
Anger, Rage, Fury	Forgiveness, Peace, Stillness
Anxiety, Fear, Worry	Calmness, Courage, Confidence
Sadness, Sorrow, Grief	Happiness, Contentment, Joy
Guilt, Shame, Embarrassment	Innocence, Feeling valued, Feeling relaxed and secure
Hurt, Disappointment	Pleasure, Satisfaction
Rejection, Estrangement, Feeling spurned	Acceptance, Feeling included, Feeling appreciated
Resentment, Blaming, Feeling judgmental	Liking, Praising, Allowing, Releasing
Hate, Disgust, Despising	Love, Delight, Admiration

Condemnation, Judgment, Blame	Absolution, Acceptance, Feeling valued, Blamelessness, Purity
Victimization, Betrayal, Deception	Winning, Support, Trust, Respect
Ridicule, Feeling put down	Admiration, Praise, Feeling elevated
Foolish, Silly, Feeling flustered	Feeling wise, dignified, and collected
Unworthiness, Failure	Worthiness, Success, Winning
Confusion, Uncertainty, Feeling lost	Clarity, Decisiveness, Focus
Feeling unsettled, stirred up, edgy	Feeling relaxed, settled, cool, calm
Feeling down, depressed, bummed out, having the blahs	Feeling up, sunny, enthusiastic, happy, energized
Emptiness, Apathy, Feeling dry	Feeling full, engaged, and juicy
Feeling overwhelmed	Being at ease, Adventurous
Feeling burned out and exhausted	Feeling recharged and energized

WELL-BEING: INHIBITORS AND ENHANCERS

Feeling good stems from cultivating a strong sense of well-being. Well-being is experienced when you believe that you have the ability to access options that feel good to you for every challenge you face. If we want to cultivate a consciousness of well-being, we need to understand what holds us back from feeling that we can face the difficulties and challenges of day-to-day living.

The way we respond to challenges can inhibit our well-being:

- × Thoughts: judgment or right/wrong thinking—we decide that something or someone is "wrong."

- × Strong desire: to make the situation or the person different.

- × Belief doesn't match our desire: We *do not believe* that we have the ability to impact the person or situation that is causing us to feel distressed.

- × Imbalance: The *disparity between desire and belief* causes an emotional imbalance within us, an internal struggle or battle.

- × Health issues: strong passionate desire without a substantial amount of belief to match it. This *imbalance* between desire and belief creates stress which negatively impacts our emotional and physical well-being. I define stress as a negative response or reaction to the hurdles in our life.

- × Feeling powerless or victimized: immobilized and incapable of creating our intentions. Identifying ourselves as victims will cause us to attract more reasons to feel like a victim, creating more reasons to feel stressed.

In an attempt to feel better we may:

- × Keep asking *why*, and analyze something over and over again.

- × Try to control others to get them to do something that makes us feel better.

- × Try to control the situation to get what we want.

✕   Try to change ourselves (perhaps stepping out of integrity) in order to give someone else what he or she wants.

✕   Point a finger of blame at self or others.

None of these ways has a positive impact on our relationships. But when we have a strong sense of well-being, we respond to the people in our lives and to day-to-day challenges differently.

10 Essentials to Well-Being

1.   Love yourself. The greater our self-love, the greater our belief in our ability to attract positive relationships, and the stronger our foundation from which to launch our desires. We cannot feel in charge of our lives if we are feeling like victims; instead, we will attract more reasons to feel that our lives are out of control. We must learn to reframe every situation by releasing judgment of self and others—which is not the same as agreeing. The more we love ourselves, the greater our capacity to build strong, healthy relationship with others.

2.   Stay in the present; put the past behind. We maintain thresholds of how much pain and how much well-being we allow into our lives. When our level for happiness starts to shift out of our comfort zone, we unconsciously attract situations and circumstances that maintain this level. The degree to which we allow things to upset us depends upon how many other pressing issues are occurring in our lives. It also depends on how many issues from the past we have stuffed into our consciousness without addressing them when they occurred.

3.   Forgive yourself and others. When we forgive ourselves or someone else, we are choosing to release our judgments. In so doing, we are choosing to feel good rather than bad, positive rather than negative, free rather than imprisoned.

4. Be grateful. Gratitude is the acknowledgement of well-being. It is a state of mind that creates the building blocks for optimal relationships. It inspires us to be and do our best. Being grateful helps us to see the gifts in our relationships and to inspire others to give more of themselves while being the best they can be.

5. Live from integrity. Decisions that are not within the highest degree of integrity will be accompanied by negative emotions. For example, when a decision feels like a sacrifice, we are not in alignment with our true selves. However, when we give freely because we want to or because it feels like the right thing to do, rather than an obligation, the emotion we feel is positive. Sacrificing leads to resentment and creates negative feelings. Giving rather than sacrificing keeps our relationships positive and open.

6. Create a consciousness of abundance. Anytime we talk about *not having enough*, we create a consciousness of scarcity and attract more of the same. Abundance is something we create in our consciousness before it appears in our reality. It is created through our willingness to see the gifts in every situation and to choose to be optimistic as we move through life's challenges. Albert Einstein put this simply when he said, "Not everything that can be counted counts, and not everything that counts can be counted."

7. Be lighthearted. Create time in your busy schedule to laugh. See humor whenever possible. Smile a lot. Notice people smiling at you. Laughter is a wonderful gift to both give and receive. Take time to use your playful imagination, seeing greater possibilities wherever you can.

8. Be optimistic. Value every experience as one from which positive changes can arise to ensure more desirable results in the future. Optimism helps us to minimize the impact of undesirable events and to focus our attention on what we can learn from the experience.

Pessimism involves reacting to undesirable events and blowing them out of proportion, taking the blame, or blaming others for the outcome. When we are optimistic, we learn from the experience; when we are pessimistic, we do not learn.

9. Use your intuition. Intuition is often referred to as a gut feeling, a knowing, a hunch. It is an inspiration or an idea that comes out of the blue. In Harmonic Matching, believing in yourself and following your intuitive guidance to inspire you into action are two key ingredients for successful relationships.

10. Correlate your thoughts, emotions, and beliefs with what you are attracting. Learning from every experience involves lining up and harmonizing our thoughts, emotions, and beliefs with what we are attracting and creating on a day-to-day basis. In this way, we can take responsibility to grow and create new experiences rather than make the same error over and over again. This is important when relating to others because our relationships are always "works in progress."

HOW TO CREATE WELL-BEING

To help the executives and the employees of the organizations where I consult to be more centered as they moved about in their busy days, I created three plans to well-being, which can be used unless contrary to your physician's advice: a 1-minute plan, a 30-minute plan, and a 60-minute plan.

The 1-minute plan, detailed in the following list, is a daily practice of shifting your consciousness to create positive emotion.

×   *Pay attention to negative emotion*, which is a sign that you need to consciously shift your thoughts in the direction of your desires.

×   When you feel negative emotion, ask yourself this question: *What new desire does this bring forth in me?*

×   Quickly focus your thoughts on the new desire instead of on the fear of not having what you want.

×   Set the intention to align your beliefs with your desire. Command your subconscious mind to help you attract reasons to believe you can have what you want ("this or something better").

×   Consciously choose to look for thoughts that feel better to you.

The 30-minute plan incorporates the 1-minute plan and adds pre-paving along with additional activities, including these daily practices:

×   Journal of intentions. Write three pages every day to pre-pave your intentions. Address your personal and work-related concerns by listing each item of concern and then writing intentions for how you want the outcome to be for each situation.

×   Pre-pave your day. Set different intentions at different times of the day. Our day is normally divided into various segments. For example, in the morning, we prepare for work (eat breakfast, shower, get dressed, and so on). Then we move into the next segment when we drive to work. A third segment begins when we walk into the office and sift through our e-mails and phone messages. Another segment begins when we attend a meeting or begin a project. Each part of the day is a new segment and deserves a new intention. Use what you know about the subconscious by setting these intentions in your mind. Perhaps as you shower in the morning you can set the intention to leave on time. As you drive to work, you may set the intention to be inspired to take the route in which traffic is flowing easily. You might also set the intention to enjoy your drive. I like to set the intention that I will drive the speed limit and that I will drive safely and be around other drivers who do the same. When you move to the next segment, responding to your e-mails, you set new intentions, which might include to respond promptly and thoughtfully. Perhaps as you are walking to your meeting, you might set the intention that you cover all items on the agenda and that you offer valuable insights.

× Sit quietly by yourself without having an agenda. Just 15 minutes every day will enhance your overall sense of well-being.

× Be grateful. Make a mental or written list of all the things you are grateful for at the end of your day.

The 60-minute plan incorporates the 1-minute plan and the thirty-minute plan along with some additional activities.

× Exercise. Go to the gym or take a walk. Do this at least 20 minutes a day, or for longer periods at least three times each week. Pay attention to what you see, hear, smell, taste, and feel. Let this be a walking meditation.

× Participate in a mind-body technique such as yoga, or get a massage. Do this at least three times each week, although daily would be even better. You can take a class or use a DVD for in-home instruction.

× Eat a healthy diet every day.

× Practice being optimistic about the challenges you experience throughout the day.

THE TRAFFIC LIGHT GUIDANCE SYSTEM

Your feelings are very important indicators of how close you are to connecting with the alignment that will bring you whatever you desire. Imagine traffic lights to direct the "traffic" of your thoughts and feelings.

Green Light—Continue Thinking as You Are

When you feel good about yourself and your life, as Hilary did when she shifted toward taking a positive action, your "feeling indicator light" is a bright green. This tells you that you are on course to "Go!" If you continue thinking as you are, you will be able to ride your inner guidance in the direction of your desires.

Yellow Light—Slow Down and Pay Attention!

When you are feeling unsettled or unfocused, your thoughts are only partially aligned with your wishes. In this case, your "feeling indicator light" is yellow. When you are not feeling clear or positive, tell yourself to slow down.

How can you get off this self-defeating frequency? Simply distract yourself by shifting your thoughts to a more positive subject. The way you do this is to ask yourself, *What new desire does this bring forth in me?* Then choose to focus your attention on the desire. Although this takes practice, it will help you move out of a place of deprivation and scarcity thinking into a more appreciative mode, which will always lift your energy to a higher level. When you replace thoughts of "I can't do it" or "I'm worthless" with thoughts that say "I intend to do this and to attract whatever I need to make it happen," a shift will take place in the physical world as well as in your mental and emotional worlds. Now is the time to become consciously more optimistic.

Red Light—Stop and Shift the Direction of Your Thoughts

When you are feeling unhappy, your thoughts are definitely out of alignment with your desires, and your "feeling indicator light" is red. Positive creativity is at a standstill, and your attention is focused on what you *do not want*. When your energy is low and your emotions are focused on negative feelings, it is difficult to attract good things into your life. As the Law of Attraction tells us, "like attracts like."

Figure 5-2

Vibrational Consciousness Resulting in Alignment with Desires

Thoughts	Beliefs	Emotions	Vibration	Experiences	Indicator Light	Action to Create a Vibrational Consciousness in Harmony with Desires
Completely in alignment with desires	In harmony with desires	Feeling fabulous	High	Attracting positive experiences	GREEN GO	Continue thinking as you are
Inconsistent alignment with desires	Inconsistent alignment with desires	Feeling "So-So"	Middle of the range: fluctuates between high and low	Attracting some positive and some negative experiences	YELLOW SLOW DOWN	• Be aware of your emotions • Ask yourself what thoughts are bringing on negative emotions • Ask yourself, *What new desire does this negative situation bring forth in me?* • Choose to focus on the new desire. • Engage in "feel good" moments or distractions
Unaligned with desires	Disharmony with desires	Feeling bad	Low	Attracting negative experiences	RED STOP & SHIFT	• Be aware of your emotions • Ask yourself what thoughts are bringing on negative emotions • Ask yourself, *What new desire does this negative situation bring forth in me?* • Choose to focus on the new desire. • Engage in "feel good" moments or distractions

Figure 5-2 shows how you can use your "feeling indicator light" to align your thoughts with your desires.

Sometimes when we begin thinking of a pleasant memory, we remember something unpleasant about it. In a matter of seconds, we shift from a positive, high-energy state (green light) to a negative, low-energy state (red light).

I remember how enthused I felt when I started my consulting business. I still have good memories about setting up my office and being awarded my first contract. A few months later my business was flowing. However, several well-meaning friends stopped by for lunch early on, and during the conversation they cautioned me about the dangers of self employment and suggested I get a part-time job to secure a consistent income. By the time they finished their lecture on the pitfalls of being an entrepreneur, I was starting to doubt my own judgment about going out on my own.

If I were to choose this memory to help me raise my state, I might start out feeling warm and fuzzy, but then, remembering my friends' lecture, I would shift to feeling cold and disheartened. I can reframe my thoughts, of course, and choose to see this situation from a higher perspective, but when I am consciously trying to raise my state to a higher level in order to attract a desire, it would be better to choose a different feel-good memory that is fully positive.

If you are a pet lover, you might choose a memory of holding and stroking your cat, dog, or rabbit as they exude pure positive energy. A happy memory like this can quickly soothe us into a pure state of positive feelings. Whatever you choose, it is good to have one or two special memories you can use, or activities that you can count on, to help you quickly shift your feelings into a higher place.

CULTIVATE OPTIMISM

One of the most empowering findings psychology has discovered in the last 30 years is that people can *choose* the way they think. The power of optimism has been well documented by Dr. Martin Seligman, author of *Learned Optimism*.

Seligman's research confirmed that an optimistic attitude has a significant impact on longevity, success on aptitude tests, good marks in school, and success at work.

> *You are wired for happiness. This may come as*
> *a surprise to you, but it's the truth.*
> — Bob Murray, PhD, and Alicia Fortinberry, MS

When we are feeling pessimistic, we take undesirable events and blow them out of proportion, taking the blame or blaming others for the outcome. On the other hand, when we are feeling optimistic, we minimize the impact of undesirable events and focus our attention on what we can learn from the experience. Every experience is valued as one from which positive changes can occur to ensure more desirable results in the future. When we consciously choose to live from an optimistic perspective, our positive energy remains strong regardless of the events that come our way. This orientation ensures a higher degree of success in achieving a positive outcome for any situation.

CLARITY OF EXPECTATIONS

When organizational leaders want to create desirable outcomes, their first step is to create a positive culture, which enhances positive feelings in their management teams and their employees. By communicating a positive vision throughout the organization, they can inspire engagement and passion for the mission.

A clear vision gives people a sense of purpose. Any new initiative needs to build good feelings that inspire employees to engage whole-heartedly in the process and that convey the message that their leaders care about them. Good feelings build up positive energy for the project and the organization. To create this state, leaders must communicate clarity of expectations.

Clarity of expectations can be integrated with project engagement by connecting these elements:

- Creating feel-good moments at the start of the project.
- Communicating clear expectations at all levels.
- Providing tools and support.
- Listening to what your employees need to accomplish the job.
- Encouraging team support and information-sharing throughout the organization.
- Respecting everyone's creative input and focusing it on the purpose.
- Coming from integrity and fostering a culture of integrity.
- Motivating by inspiring rather than attempting to force engagement.
- Defining clear agreements.
- Expecting people to hold themselves accountable.
- Showing appreciation by rewarding team work, innovation, and productivity.

Most employees want to do a good job and derive satisfaction from doing so. Establishing clarity of expectations with integrity keeps people focused on creating positive outcomes.

It is also important to remember that employees respond more to what you *do* than to what you *say*. If you say that you value one thing, but reward something else, they will do what you reward and what you spend time on, rather than what you only give lip service to.

~~~

Inspiring is about creating feel-good moments that motivate people with passion and purpose. This is the key to step one in the Harmonic Matching Process. You can apply this understanding in professional relationships and personal relationships. The people you relate to will be attracted to the positive energy you create and will be engaged when you create clarity about what you expect.

DO YOUR THOUGHTS ENHANCE OR INHIBIT POSITIVE RELATIONSHIPS?

If you are thinking good thoughts about your relationships, they will be enhanced. If you are thinking pessimistic thoughts, your relationships will be inhibited. Negative thoughts create resistance to attracting positive relationships—but the wonderful discovery is that you can *choose* to guide your thoughts in more and more positive directions. The result will be increasingly enhanced relationships and new opportunities.

When you combine positive thoughts with good feelings on a regular basis, you build up enhancing habits in the same way that regular exercise builds up muscles. This establishes powerful beliefs that attract your desires into being.

When you are fearful of a negative outcome, your attention to it attracts that outcome to you. But as you intentionally build up self-esteem and habits of thinking and feeling lovingly toward yourself, you lower your resistance to attracting your desires. The more optimistic you are, the quicker your desires will manifest. You can change inhibition into enhancement.

By creating feel-good moments in your present relationships and focusing on feel-good memories from your life, you build up your resource pool of positive emotions. When you connect those good feelings with optimistic thoughts about your desires, you direct your subconscious to attract them into reality.

HOW A LEADER ENHANCED HIS STYLE

After doing a 360-degree Evaluation process for a large healthcare system, I was brought in to do executive coaching with some of the top staff, including Richard, a senior vice president in the organization. In our initial meeting, he set a goal of wanting to improve staff retention because several desirable key people had recently left. As we talked in the coaching sessions, Richard admitted that people were frustrated by his communication style. He realized that many of them saw him as abrupt, cut-and-dry, and not soliciting enough input from his management team. Some felt that he didn't listen to their ideas.

"I sometimes get the sense that they don't trust me," Richard told me. That was a point that had come out in the 360-degree Evaluation, and he admitted that he had heard this before; it wasn't exactly news to him. I asked him, "Do you think it is important how your management team feels about your style?" He really didn't think it was. Then I asked, "Do you think you can lead if you have no following?" As he thought about this, I could see that he was beginning to get the point and was becoming open to a shift in perspective. I added, "It may not matter if they like you, but they must respect you and feel that you respect them. Would you follow someone you felt didn't respect and care about you? Or would you look for another job?" I was guiding him to make a shift to a better way of achieving his desires (better staff retention) by considering the perspectives of other people.

As we continued to work together, it was clear that he was cognizant that it is important to have a following in order to be a leader. Richard came to understand that his people wanted him to be more sensitive to their emotions and not be so curt. When he attempted to hold people accountable, they felt as though he was grabbing them by the collar, and felt put off. One employee had said, "What makes him think that I don't hold myself accountable to the agreements I made?" As a result of these realizations, Richard understood that he had to show his team that he did care about them. He shifted his style to be more sensitive and more supportive.

Six months later, after a follow-up Organizational Culture Analysis, people were noticing that Richard was trying. He was making progress. They said that they felt he was more sensitive, that he appreciated and respected them more, and that he now solicited their ideas and input to a much greater degree. Richard had begun to create more feel-good moments for his employees by his greater appreciation, by deeper listening, and by greater awareness of their perspectives. The result was that Richard was able to demonstrate to the CEO that he was able to inspire his management team to engage the new organizational vision with passion and purpose. Staff retention in his department had also markedly improved.

Every successful leader wants to be more effective, even if it means stretching beyond one's comfort zone to learn new skills.

TRANSFORMATIONAL BOOSTERS TO CREATE FEEL-GOOD MOMENTS

× Inspiring instead of demanding. It is much easier to get excellent creative work from people when they *want* to give it than when they feel they *have* to.

× Setting clear expectations. A clear plan of action gives people confidence that they know what you want. This empowers them and helps them feel good about engaging the project with their full capacities.

× Focusing creativity. Instead of fearing that creativity will go off on a tangent, guide it by focusing people's creative energy in the direction of desirable outcomes.

× Setting positive intentions. When we create a good feeling about the desirability of the intention we are stating, we engage energetic, positive support to achieve it.

× Generating enthusiasm. Persuade people to engage your desires by helping them to understand the purpose.

× Reminding people of their past successes. When you help others see themselves as successful, you inspire them to reach for new successes by enhancing positive beliefs.

× Explaining the purpose of an action. Help people feel that they are part of the plan by sharing the reasons why things have to be done a certain way. This helps people feel that they are valued members of the team. Share the information that helps them do a good job of accomplishing the purpose you intend.

× Asking for and valuing input. When you sincerely ask someone, "What do you think?" it makes them feel that their intelligence and creativity are respected. This creates a feel-good moment between you.

× Appreciating people. Everyone desires to be seen and appreciated. Stating your appreciation costs so little and is one of the most effective ways of motivating people to create even more positive and successful relationships and opportunities.

× Rewarding people with feel-good moments. A smile, a wave, a kind word, a thank-you—these small gestures raise emotional energy and help relationships grow and prosper.

× Letting people know you care about them. Relating to people is not a one-way street. Try to understand how things look from other people's points of view. Let them know you are aware of what is going on in their lives and that they matter as people, not just as tools to achieve your objectives. To build trust between you, listen to them.

×　Redefining "problems" as "challenges. Shifting the perspective from inhibiting negative emotions to positive and optimistic emotions turn barriers into adventures that can be overcome.

AT A GLANCE: A SUMMARY OF STEP ONE OF THE HARMONIC MATCHING PROCESS

1. Creating feel-good moments generates energy to build positive relationships and opportunities.

2. Building up a store of positive emotions and relationships is the first step in the Harmonic Matching process.

3. Use your most positive memories to lift your emotions into a resourceful state.

4. Value yourself. When your confidence and self-esteem are high, you attract positive relationships.

5. The Law of Attraction states: *like attracts like*.

6. You can shift your emotions from negative to positive by realigning your thoughts.

7. Emotional transformation shifts your focus from fearing that you will not have something you want to believing in your ability to attract what you desire.

8. You attract into your life exactly what you believe you will attract.

9. Your subconscious mind obeys your beliefs and manifests them for you.

10. Your emotions provide a guidance system to tell you when your thoughts and beliefs are or are not in alignment with your desires.

11. Optimism is a winner. The more optimistic you are, the quicker your desires manifest. Shifting to an optimistic view reduces resistance, enhances your

relationships, and attracts new options and opportunities.

12. To create positive relationships, establish clarity of expectations among the people you interact with. Then show appreciation for harmonic co-creative efforts.

13. Remember, to bring resources, opportunities, and relationships to you, you must develop the skill of correlating your thoughts, beliefs, and emotions with what you are attracting. In this way, you will learn from every experience and strengthen your attraction power. (More on this in Chapters 7 and 8.)

Step one of the Harmonic Matching Process shows you how creating feel-good moments in your personal and professional life attracts successful relationships and opportunities. Feel-good moments provide the positive emotional energy to build and achieve the relationship goals you will learn about in the next chapter.

CHAPTER SIX

STEP TWO:
Identify Your Desires

*You need to consciously decide what you want, because knowing
what you want determines what you will get. Before something
happens in the external world, it must first happen in the
internal world. There is something rather amazing about
what happens when you get a clear representation of what you
want. It programs your mind and body to achieve that goal.*

—Anthony Robbins

Step two in the Harmonic Matching Process focuses on
the importance of identifying your desires and defining
your relationship goals. Almost everything we want in
life comes to us through relationships. *The Relationship Code*
guides you to create clear relationship goals for all parts of
your life—personal and professional—and shows you how to
focus on what you want rather than giving attention to what
you *do not* want.

WISH LISTS: WHAT RELATIONSHIPS DO YOU WANT?

How do you want your primary relationships to be? Almost everything we could desire in life comes through relationships with others. Before we can successfully attract positive relationships, we have to think about what we want, and create clear relationship goals.

In step two, you should put aside all thoughts about what you think is "realistic" or "achievable." This step is about *what you truly desire*. If you limit your dreams before you even begin, how can you attract what you really want? First identify what you want, whether you believe it is possible or not. Later we will talk about how to get there. You certainly cannot attain your desires if you do not know what they are.

Do you want a good job? One critical component of a good job is your relationship with the person you report to. What kind of relationship do you want with your ideal boss? Have you thought about what you want from a boss? If you have people reporting to you, what do you want from your team?

Do you want to find a loving partner or enhance the relationship you have with your significant other? What kind of couple relationship do you want? What kind of relationship do you want with your friends? To build great relationships, we have to pay attention to them and think about what we desire. If we don't consciously set positive intentions for our relationships, they will be unconsciously defined by old habit patterns and expectations from our subconscious.

Tips for creating wish lists:

- × Think and dream before you write. Reach for the most positive desire you can imagine—then ask yourself how you could make it even better.

- × If the first thoughts that come are about what you *don't* want, write them on a separate piece of paper. When you begin to create your wish list, reverse these negative thoughts into positive statements about what you *do* want. Change "I don't want a boss who yells at me" into "I want a boss who is kind and helpful to me."

×   Push aside self-sabotaging, negative thoughts about what you can't have. You deserve to know what you truly desire. Allowing yourself to feel your desires is more than halfway to attracting them. Simply creating your relationship goals sets up a field of energy that brings them closer to you.

×   Be sure that the wishes you write are your own, not what you think you should want or what someone else wants you to want.

×   Begin and end your wish lists with a written intention that the fulfillment of your wishes be for the highest good of all concerned.

For the Highest Good of All

One client of mine had a wish list on which he wrote that he wanted his boss to see him as competent. He had not said anything about being appreciated or rewarded, but he did add "for the highest good of all" at the end. As a result, he got it all, much more than he had even imagined. By creating this wish list, he was inspired to take on an additional project, which required working a few weekends. When he completed the project, his boss did see him as competent. His boss also expressed whole-hearted appreciation for his work. When you wish the best for everyone, as well as yourself, you attract the possibility of greater benefits than you could have thought of by yourself.

Sometimes, although you may not get the thing you thought you wanted, because you asked for the highest good you open the door to getting something far better. To receive your highest good, stay open to new relationships and opportunities that can fulfill your intentions even better than anything you could have dreamed up. Create your goals as clearly as possible, but remain open to something even better.

The wish lists on the following pages help you set clear relationship goals. You can use these to attract new relationships or to enhance an existing relationship. Remember, these are just samples to get you started. Look within yourself to find out exactly and specifically what you personally desire.

Boss Relationship Wish List

Who does not want a good relationship with his boss? Everyone reports to someone. Even the CEO of a large organization reports to shareholders and major customers. When you get clear about what you want in a boss, you begin to align yourself with the position that best fits your desires. Here are some examples of what people may want from a boss:

× I want a boss who cares about me as a person.

× I want a boss who appreciates my talents and skill set.

× I want a boss who listens to my ideas and creative input.

× I want a boss who supports my work by providing the things I need.

× I want a boss who trusts me enough to help me understand the organizational politics and who guides me so I can be of better help to her or him.

× I want my boss to mentor me and help me grow in the organization.

× I want my boss to understand the difficulties of my personal situation.

× I want my boss to encourage me and help me deal with a challenging project.

× I want my boss to be kind, gentle, and inspiring.

× I want to work for a boss who is ambitious and wants to bring me along as he or she climbs the corporate ladder.

× I want all of the above, or whatever is for my highest good and the highest good for all concerned.

I once coached Mark, a manager who felt that his boss wasn't supporting him. As we talked about the situation, it became clear that he was attracting criticism because he was expecting criticism. By helping him develop a more positive idea of what he wanted from his boss, I was able to help Mark think about the relationship in a whole new way. As he began to project his true desires for the relationship, his boss started to respond in a new way that reflected Mark's more positive attitude. For the first time, Mark began to see the possibility of consciously creating his relationship goals as a necessary step toward achieving them.

Leader's Team Relationships Wish List

Most people have some situation in which they are the leader, either formally in an organization or informally in a social group. As leaders, we want to build strong teams who are committed to us and the organization and who respond to our guidance and direction while giving valuable input for decision-making. Here are some things people may want from the people they lead:

- ✕   I want a harmonious team that gets along well internally.

- ✕   I want a team that stays focused on the task at hand.

- ✕   I want team members who bring all their talents to the table and go the extra mile to do an excellent job.

- ✕   I want the most able members of my team to follow my lead. I want them to stay in alignment with my vision and to fully support it.

- ✕   I want team members who respect my leadership and listen to my guidance.

- ✕   I want team members who are flexible and will fill in gaps for me where needed.

- ✕   I want team members who can think creatively and bring new ideas to the table.

×   I want team members who are solution-oriented and hold themselves highly accountable for doing a fabulous job.

×   I want everyone on my team to be more productive.

×   I want team members who have the highest degree of integrity.

×   I want team members who are extremely competent and foster a spirit of cooperation and innovativeness.

×   I want all of the above, or whatever is for my highest good and the highest good for all concerned.

When I was coaching David, a leader in a large healthcare organization, he identified several things that irked him about the people who reported to him. He felt that many of the people on his team weren't following through on their agreements and that they were not giving their best energies to the group effort.

As David worked on his wish list, I suggested that he begin by listing the qualities that he *liked* about his team. He noted a couple of team members whom he felt had been creative and engaged, and in particular one key person who had shown true loyalty to his vision. This put him in a grateful and positive state that flowed into his list as he wrote down the positive wishes he had for better productivity from the rest of the team. David realized that putting his relationship goals for his team into positive terms was helping him feel more confident about the possibility of change. He began to think creatively and positively about how to achieve his desired goals.

CREATING VERSUS MIS-CREATING YOUR DESIRES

Your emotions reflect what you are holding in your consciousness. Thoughts that have strong emotions attached to them, coupled with your strong belief in them, create a very powerful force for drawing things into your experience. If you are drawing something you desire into your experience, you will feel good. If you are drawing something into your experience that is not aligned with your desires, you will have negative emotions. Pay attention to your feelings—they will give you feedback regarding whether or not you are attracting and creating experiences aligned with your deepest desires. When we feel good, our thoughts and beliefs about a specific situation are in alignment with what we want. When we feel bad (worried, anxious, sad, and so on), our thoughts and beliefs about a specific topic are out of alignment with our desires.

Our feelings about ourselves are the foundation for the experiences we attract. Because what we give attention to shows up in our experience, whatever we believe about ourselves is confirmed over and over again.

We cannot attract a supportive boss if we feel unsupported or hold the idea of lack of support in our consciousness. What we attract are more reasons to feel isolated and unsupported by the people around us.

We cannot attract team members who hold themselves accountable if we feel (hold in our consciousness) that the people we deal with are irresponsible. Instead, we attract more reasons to feel that we cannot count on the people around us.

We cannot create good friendships if we feel (hold in our consciousness) lonely. Instead we attract more reasons to feel isolated.

We cannot attract a loving intimate partner if we feel (hold in our consciousness) unloved. Instead we attract more reasons to feel unlovable.

Remember, whatever you believe about yourself and others, and therefore feel about yourself and others, is a signal to your subconscious to attract more of the same.

Therefore, to shift toward our goals and desires, we must create a new diet of self-talk that reassures us we are in harmony with whatever we want to attract and reinforces the idea that the people in our lives represent what we want to create more of in our experience. Once we have raised our vibrational consciousness, we can move more confidently toward attracting a desirable harmonic match. The way to do this is to set an intention to feel good about ourselves in every way, including the gifts we can bring to a relationship.

THE PROCESS OF IDENTIFYING RELATIONSHIP DESIRES

Getting clear about what we want in our relationships often requires us to work through various barriers to knowing our true desires. By learning about what is standing in our way, we can cut through the barriers and create clear goals. We can use visualization processes to help us know what we want and be able to write processes to clarify the wording of our goals to attract positive outcomes for everyone involved. The process of identifying and defining goals aligns us with a proactive, rather than reactive orientation that is always better for attracting the results we want.

Using Imagery to Clarify Your Goals

Visual imagination is a powerful tool for developing positive relationship goals. Place your hand on your heart and press firmly to connect your head and your heart. Take several deep and soothing breaths before you begin your visualization session.

Picture the person you are relating to, either someone you know or someone new that you hope to attract into your life. See that person relating to you in the positive ways you desire. Visualize that person as smiling and happy as she interacts with you. You can create an inner movie of your desired relationship and feel the pleasure it brings to both of you.

If negative images arise, turn down the lighting and the sound and let that image fade away, getting smaller and dimmer as it goes. Fill the visual space with happy images in bright and pleasing colors. Picture yourself with your friends, your teammates, or your boss in a beautiful setting. For example, imagine you could take your whole work team to a lovely restaurant beside a lake. Picture the sunset shining on the water as everyone is gathering for a meal on the deck overlooking the harbor. Visualize harmony and laughter around the table and see everyone smiling at you. You might add an award ceremony to commemorate a project successfully completed. You could see your boss there, thanking you for leading the team so well.

Notice the specific details of your visualizations that give you the best feelings. Search out images on the Internet or in magazine illustrations that capture those images. Begin a collection of images for your vision board. This is a private representation of the visual images that best represent the relationship goals you visualize. You can put these images on a bulletin board in a place where only you can see it; for example, in a private study, covered by a cloth, or in a secure folder on your personal computer. It is important to keep these images private because they create an internal conversation that you have with your subconscious. You do not want anyone else's comments or opinions, even positive ones, becoming part of your inner dialogue.

Each time you visualize or look at your vision board, think of ways to make the images more pleasing to you. This is another element of your inner dialogue with your mind, and there are no limits to how beautiful you can make your images. Palaces, gardens, rainbows, boats—add any image that makes you feel good, happy, and successful. Your imagination is free to create any image. Creating these images will take you closer to your desires and help you become better able to write down what you want on your wish lists.

Writing Relationship Desires

Get into the habit of regularly writing down and refining your relationship desires. This will help you get clearer about exactly what you want. Here are some tips for writing your list:

×   Write your desires as clearly and precisely as you can.

×   Make your list as specific as possible. Start with the general idea and add details until it feels right to you—it needs to truly state what you want.

×   Focus on *what you do want*, not on what you *don't* want. Change all negative statements and feelings into positive ones. Every negative has many opposite positives.

×   Don't focus on what you think is "realistic" in this step. Here you are finding out what you desire. It doesn't matter whether you believe that the goal is achievable or not, just whether it is exactly what you want.

×   When your desire is clear, every part of you will be in agreement. "That is 100 percent what I want. I have no reservations or resistance. If it came true right now, I would be completely happy with it."

Intending the Highest Good for All Concerned

Every relationship desire involves other people. By setting your intentions for the highest good of all concerned, you allow your subconscious mind to attract even better relationships than you can imagine. By keeping our intentions focused on the highest good for all, we maximize the positive energy and minimize resistance to our desires. If you ignore the well-being of others and focus only on your own desires, you subconsciously stir up resistance to achieving what you want. By intending the highest good, both for yourself and for everyone else, you send out signals that attract a positive outcome supported by all.

Begin and end every wish list and every visualization exercise with a strong intention, which you say to yourself and write down, that these wishes be fulfilled.

COMMUNICATING RELATIONSHIP GOALS TO OTHERS

Relationships are essentially dialogues with other people. They move along a two-way street, both giving and receiving.

After you have done the private work of developing your relationship goals, you need to find effective ways of communicating them to others. Remember, other people are looking for positive relationships too. Here are some tips on communicating goals:

× Use words and ideas to which other people relate. Strive to inspire their interest and participation.

× Ask questions about what others want out of the relationship. Try to avoid relying on assumptions by asking respectful questions to find out if your assumptions are true. For example: "It occurred to me that you may be concerned about x and that you may want y. Have I understood your perspective, or are there other concerns you want to tell me about?"

× Listen closely for key words and phrases that help you understand how others see the situation, what they may want, and what they may fear. Demonstrate that you care about their highest good as well as your own.

× Negotiate in good faith. Cultivate trust by coming from integrity and clarity.

× Create clear written agreements. Be sure that they are mutually agreed to and that all parties have had a hand in expressing what is feasible for them. Work to make sure your agreements are fair, and represent, to the best of your ability, the highest good for all concerned. Even close friends will benefit from written agreements about anything involving money or serious commitments. It is better to be clear at the beginning than lose a friend over a misunderstanding.

The Structure of Agreements

Although agreements can have many structures and forms, some key components need to be part of almost any agreement involving co-creative work or relationship-building. Rather than looking at the details of legal contracts or project management documents, here we are exploring the broader principles and reasons how and why well-formed agreements work. Well-formed agreements minimize misunderstandings and enhance the co-creative effort of each party.

There are similarities and differences between professional and personal agreements; the better you understand the way agreements work and the reasons for particular elements, the more effectively you will be able to communicate fair and positive agreements that help to attract and develop positive relationships.

Professional Agreements

Professional agreements usually focus on the facts of what a group work effort will involve. Though there are many kinds of agreements, and every organization develops its own structures and processes, most professional agreements require some form of the following components:

× Purpose.

× Scope of work.

× Deliverables and requirements.

× Schedule.

× Budget.

× Resources required.

× Roles and responsibilities.

Before an organization sets out to meet the goals of a particular project, it needs to define clearly what its purposes are. It may seem obvious that defining the purpose of a project is necessary, but too often the focus goes quickly to the details, and the bigger picture is forgotten. Executives should not assume that everyone in the organization will understand why the project is being launched or that everyone on the leadership team has the same idea. When a clear statement of purpose is written down and input is gathered from the leadership team, many misunderstandings can be avoided.

Every agreement should clearly define the scope of the project, program, or initiative, including what is outside its scope. Many programs fail because of a well-known problem called "scope creep," or "mission creep." When any group of people get together to do something, there will be many varying points of view about what is most important. This results in a tendency to add more scope to the effort than its schedule and budget can bear. By defining the scope of the project as clearly as possible, decision-makers have a baseline against which to decide whether to add time and money to accommodate the proposed expansion or not. If such clear decisions are not made, team members begin to lose trust in the integrity of the process, and a free-for-all may result, with each manager trying to get as much of the ill-defined scope (and budgeted funds) shifted his way as possible.

The agreement should state clearly what the product deliverables will be and give some definition of what they are required to contain. A definition of requirements often gives specific measurable criteria for determining if the deliverable meets expectations.

Every agreement that involves work produced over time needs to have a schedule setting forth when resources are needed and when deliverables will be completed. A good schedule usually has interim milestones that define phases of completion and ways of determining if the initiative is on schedule or not so that early corrective measures can be taken, if necessary. A clear schedule also allows team members to break down the work into small increments and check their own progress to hold themselves accountable or to ask for guidance if their schedule is slipping for some reason. Managers should keep track of how the teams reporting to them are doing and correct problems as early as possible.

Every project involves costs that must be planned for in a budget. When scope, schedule, and resources have been clearly defined, the required budget should be easy to calculate. It should also make sense. In many organizations, the practice of under-budgeting and over-scoping is widespread. Although it is true that new money is often found for projects once they are under way, making this standard practice in an organization tends to erode trust and encourage game-playing within the organizational bureaucracy. Some of these practices may be unavoidable, but to the extent that senior management cultivates clear and open budgeting, they will encourage a culture of integrity, which provides a competitive advantage by simplifying the financial accounting process and by keeping the effort focused on well-defined goals.

Every agreement guiding a group work effort must define and account for the resources that will be required to do the job, including how much time is needed from each person or skill category, and how much equipment time and raw materials (and so forth) are required. One requirement that can easily get overlooked is the amount of executive oversight and review time the project will need.

The agreement also needs to define clear roles and responsibilities for all the people who will be involved, both in the day-to-day work and non-staff people in oversight positions or brought in as consulting specialists.

Well-defined agreements are one of the most critical components in ensuring the success of a group work effort. They also go a long way toward building and maintaining positive and productive work relationships.

Personal Agreements

The agreements we make in our personal relationships are generally less formal and usually involve fewer people—often just two. Personal agreements also often involve more intangibles than project agreements do. Whereas specific problem-solving dialogues work best when they focus on the specifics of a present situation, they are inevitably colored by past experience that may come into the discussion. As with all relationships, mutual respect and trust are the magic ingredients that make all agreements work better.

Sometimes personal agreements are just a matter of talking things out, but if they involve money, property, or significant commitments of work, they will work much better if they are clearly written down. Here are some of the elements to consider in writing personal agreements:

×   Dialogue and communication.

×   Respect and trust.

×   Positive humor.

×   Focus on present specifics.

×   Finding workable solutions.

×   Roles, identities, and self understanding.

×   Changing relationships.

×   Loving kindness and positive focus.

Even though you may have a clear idea of what you want from a personal relationship, remember that it is a relationship; in other words, it must be based on mutual agreement developed through dialogue and communication. Try to understand what the other person wants by asking questions and listening to what the other person has to say. All good relationships are based on respect and trust.

Even though personal relationships generally build up a rich history of experience, when you are trying to work out a specific problem, it is best to focus on the immediate issue.

Past issues should only be brought up to the degree that they are directly related to the matter at hand. A peaceful discussion about family finances can turn into an unproductive argument if old issues about other topics keep getting dragged in. Try to avoid phrases such as "You always..." or "You never...." Better to keep it focused: "When X happened, I felt Y."

Look for a workable solution that allows both people the freedom to do things in the way that best suits them. The more we come to understand ourselves, the less attached we become to controlling others in an attempt to get them to do what we want them to do. As a result, we can learn to allow the people we love the freedom to grow and discover new aspects of their lives.

Accountability and Integrity

Here are some basic principles of accountability and integrity:

×   Force is a temporary solution that leads only to a dead end. You cannot force your will on others. You *can* create the framework and provide the tools and the support to enhance accountability.

×   Inspiration and appreciation are very powerful.

×   Every agreement is a two-way street.

×   It is important to respect the fact that others want to hold themselves accountable to their agreements. When you respect others, they are likely to respond to you more positively.

×   Accountability is an internal process. It is a choice each individual makes to live up to his or her own integrity, or not. It cannot really be imposed from without. You *can* respond to someone's lack of accountability or integrity by making decisions about the relationship.

×   It is important to build into your agreements easy ways for every person involved to check and evaluate her own accountability on a daily basis.

× To attract and inspire integrity from others, we must live in integrity ourselves.

Transformational Boosters to Create Relationship Goals

The following transformational boosters can support you as you create positive goals:

× Love yourself enough to find out what you truly want. Dedicate time to discovering your truest desires.

× Dream big. Create relationship desires that inspire you.

× Think about every area of your life where you want to attract new relationships or enhance existing ones.

× Write desires that are clear. Use words that energize your feelings.

× Write goals that appeal to all five senses and are filled with specific details.

× Write goals that have measurable outcomes.

× Create goals with definite time lines by which they will be achieved.

× Improve your relationships by getting to know yourself better.

× Learn to communicate effectively with the people to whom you relate.

× Learn to be a better listener.

× Remember that a relationship involves two people.

× Relationships are nurtured by integrity, trust, respect, and love. The more of these and other good qualities you develop within yourself, the more you will attract them from others.

AT-A-GLANCE REFERENCE GUIDE

Review this summary of what you learned in step two about identifying your relationship desires:

- × Develop your relationship goals by creating written wish lists for each type of relationship you want in every area of your life, both professional and personal.

- × Set the intention for all goals to be fulfilled for the highest good of all.

- × Learn to overcome the barriers to knowing what you want by seeing through the conditioning that has told you to want something other than your heart's desire.

- × Use visual imagery to help find what you most want and increase the positive emotions associated with your goals.

- × Identify ways to make your relationship goals clear and specific. Write them down.

- × Communicate your goals with others and learn to discuss and negotiate mutually beneficial agreements.

- × Identify the components of successful professional agreements and the reasons why each component is important to define clearly.

- × Discover the elements of personal agreements. Identify ways to improve positive relationships.

Well-defined desires and relationship goals are the second step of the Harmonic Matching Process. All four steps are needed to manifest your relationship desires.

In step three, described in the next chapter, you will learn about activating your intentions and building the staircase from your wish list to the achievement of your vision.

CHAPTER SEVEN

STEP THREE:
Activate Your Intentions

First, by acting with confidence, leaders tend to inspire their followers to believe in them. In other words, confidence begets trust and confidence from others. Second, confident individuals are more likely to exhibit certain desirable behavior patterns. For example, confident leaders are action-oriented. They confront issues head on. They resolve unfinished business. They don't let conflicts linger. They deal with their fears. They push themselves to achieve their goals.

—Brian Billick

This chapter explains how important it is to blend desire and belief to activate your intentions and achieve success with the Harmonic Matching Process. I define *intention* as "strong desire coupled with strong belief." Our ability to attract depends upon the strength of our desire and our belief that we can have what we want in life. The greater the strength of the passion we feel about wanting something—coupled with the belief that we can have it—the stronger our attraction power. This power brings us closer to being a harmonic match for our desire.

A strong desire coupled with the fear of *not* having what we want, however, inhibits our attraction power. We are now a harmonic match for what we *don't* want. Step three reminds us of the necessity to make a shift from negative beliefs to positive beliefs to activate our intentions and attract the results we truly desire.

TRANSFORM AFFIRMATIONS INTO BELIEVABLE DESIRES

Step three guides us to transform the wishes we developed in step two into believable desires. Until we have activated our intentions, an affirmation may be only a wish. It may not be something we have full faith in if it is not aligned with our belief system. As a result, we may *mis-create* and attract the thing we fear or the opposite of what we desire. Until we understand the importance of all steps in the Harmonic Matching Process, we may think we have failed. This can happen when people are focusing on affirmations they don't really believe or desires that are not really their own.

If on some level we are resisting our desires, we cannot attract what we want. For example, we might be afraid of moving out of our familiar comfort zone, such as leaving a job we've had for five years. When simply wishing does not produce the result we said we wanted, we may fall into victim consciousness by putting the blame on someone else: *"They" won't let me have what I want.* This kind of thinking keeps us trapped in a victim mindset and blocks us from achieving what we really want.

ALIGN YOUR SELF-TALK TO WHAT YOU TRULY WANT

If you are outwardly saying one thing but vibrationally projecting something else that reflects your beliefs, you will attract what you are vibrationally projecting. What you are saying may not be aligned with your vibrational consciousness. The reason the words in our affirmations are important is because they reinforce positive vibrational consciousness and strengthen our belief systems to attract our desires.

By exploring your coping mechanisms and your belief systems, you can learn to notice when you are generating secret negative self-talk. As you become more self-aware, you can consciously transform negative self-talk into positive self-talk that is aligned with your desired goals. To engage the challenge and move your intentions from the wishing stage to the believable and achievable stage, you can gain empowerment through the following steps:

× **Being aware of the big picture.** When you understand how your wishes fit in to your long-term vision or goals, you can be empowered to persevere through trials and tribulations to achieve them. Also, by understanding your past—seeing how and why you have blocked your own progress—you can clarify what you really want and move toward determination and belief.

× **Reaching your decision point.** At some point, when you decide to be true to yourself rather than letting your own drama or the drama of others impede your progress, you see that achieving your vision becomes your priority. It takes precedence over the things you allowed to get in the way in the past. Now you choose to make a decision to step out of your cozy and familiar comfort zone. Now you dare to reach for what you truly want.

× **Learning from undesirable outcomes.** Most people think of undesirable outcomes as failures. If you are open to learning, however, you soon see that "failure" is not failure at all. You are just discovering what does not work. You are taking another step toward what does work.

× **Connecting your feel-good moments with your desires.** By focusing positive emotions on what it will feel like to have what you want, you are aligning your consciousness to attract your desires into your life.

× **Making positive self-talk.** When you pay attention to how you talk to yourself and others about your goals, your capabilities, and your beliefs, you can transform your self-talk into language that strengthens your belief system.

× **Focusing wishes into believable goals and objectives.** As you shift your focus to creating the staircase of goals and objectives (see Figure 7-1 later in this ccccchapter) leading from your wishes to your vision, you will find that your wishes become more refined and focused—and, in the process, more believable and achievable.

× **Finding new options.** The process of building your staircase aligns your consciousness with your desires. When you build faith in the believability of your wishes, you release struggle and attract new options that bring your desires to you more easily.

Elevate Your Beliefs

I often ask people with whom I am working, *On a scale of 1 to 10, how much do you believe you can have what you want?* If their belief in their big goal (their vision) is only at a 4, for example, I work with them to create smaller goals and objectives that lead to their bigger goal or vision. They may be able to have a strong belief in a smaller goal that is one step away from their bigger goal. I ask, *What seems believable to you?* The point is always to elevate their belief by degrees.

When you are working in step three to *activate your intentions*, start with what you can easily believe, then stretch your consciousness by considering as many options as you can imagine. Write a list of things that help you believe in your goal. Here are some examples to get you started:

× Focusing on the next step in my career path.

× Taking classes to help me advance.

× Increasing knowledge through self-study.

× Creating a plan or staircase toward my big goals or vision.

× Selling something related to one of my hobbies.

× Getting advice from people who have already achieved what I want.

The attraction process works by aligning your most passionate desires with your beliefs. It is important to create a plan or staircase to move your wishes to a higher level of believability. In this way, you are creating a vibrational consciousness in alignment with your desires. This will open up more options than you could have foreseen before.

Let's use this metaphor: Imagine that you have climbed up two steps on your staircase and suddenly you find yourself on a landing with an escalator in front of you, an elevator to your right, and several other staircases leading off in other directions. When you align your consciousness with your true desire, you have opened up new possibilities—the new staircases and the elevator. You may even be able to ride up part of the way and skip several steps. It is not simply a matter of creating a plan and laboriously carrying it out. Elevating your belief to be on the same level as what you want and staying open to opportunities creates a vibrational consciousness aligned with extraordinary opportunities and events.

Overcome Inhibitors

Most of us have acquired various inhibiting beliefs in the natural course of our lives. We may have beliefs about unworthiness, lack of capability, weakness, or opposition that trap us in the victim role. These beliefs are not objectively true; they have been conditioned into us by various life experiences. They become inhibitors because our subconscious is always working to help us affirm our beliefs about ourselves and about others. However, every human being has the choice to overcome his inhibitors by replacing beliefs that no longer serve him.

You can develop deeper self-understanding of the conditioned inhibitors that are blocking you from achieving your desired goals. Limiting beliefs can be transformed. Here are some inhibitors you can overcome:

× Habitually focusing on things that feel bad, rather than on things that feel good.

× Paying attention to what you don't have, rather than being appreciative of what you do have and being grateful for the possibilities before you.

× Being stuck in fear, anger, and shame, rather than allowing courage, calm, and confidence let you enjoy the process of moving toward your desired goals.

× Being discouraged. This minimizes your desire and belief that you can have what you want.

× Being pessimistic about your present life circumstances, rather than optimistic about both your present life circumstances and the unlimited possibilities available to you.

× Believing in scarcity and limitation, rather than in abundance and freedom.

× Staying attached to a victim identity, instead of opening up to a creative identity.

Every human being has the ability to choose. With that ability, however, comes the responsibility to overcome your inhibiting beliefs.

If you are still attached to believing in scarcity, you have to ask yourself where all the good things in your life came from. Every human advance came from someone who believed in possibilities that did not yet exist. The food in your refrigerator—and the refrigerator itself—would not exist if someone had not believed in the possibilities of keeping food fresh. All of the industries that we take for granted today came from people who believed in creating new solutions to old problems. Without someone's belief in the great abundance of life, there would be no books and no Internet.

You have the opportunity to embrace the positive choice, and the Harmonic Matching Process gives you the tools to make that choice. What should you do? Listen to your secret self-talk. Train yourself to use positive language. Avoid owning negatives by associating them with possessive language. Instead of saying, "*I am* not capable," or "It is a problem *I have*," use positive transformative language: "I am capable and I'm sure I'll find a way if I just keep at it because I always do!" "The obstacles in front of me will help me learn new things and grow." Train yourself not to connect the words *I am* with anything negative but always with something positive. Speak to yourself in language that reminds you of the transformative power of time. Every feeling is temporary and any negative can be replaced by a positive. Think and speak about every condition as something that is in transition and moving toward something better. Absolutely anything can be looked at as an opportunity for positive creativity.

Notice how your subconscious creates your reality based on your beliefs. You can allow it to go on creating your life experience based on the identity patterns you have been conditioned into, or you can choose to command your subconscious to create what you want. Everyone can learn to overcome inhibitors that have been blocking their way.

Do you want to live believing you can have what you want, or remain stuck believing you cannot have what you want? *You can choose to change your mind*. You are in control of your thoughts. Remember, your emotions make up the guidance system that tells you if your thoughts are moving in the direction of your desires or in the direction of your fears. When you are feeling good (content, happy, satisfied, and so on), your thoughts and beliefs are in alignment with what you want. Whenever you are feeling bad (anxious, hurt, angry, sad, and so on), your thoughts are in alignment with your fears.

You can enhance the power of your positive beliefs by creating believable scenarios. Remember to align your big desires with the belief necessary to achieve them by creating a staircase of goals and objectives leading you to your bigger desires. This is not settling for something less; it is moving forward one step at a time.

Create passionate intentions to *enhance your whole belief system*, not just one specific goal. Make the intention to enhance your belief that you are increasingly *capable of believing* in your goals, that your faith in your goals can become stronger.

Your subconscious does not know whether you are living something now or whether you are looking at your past or future. It does not know if you are living something today or merely fantasizing and imagining. The subconscious does not critique or judge your experiences or your beliefs. It simply knows how to bring you more of what you are aligned with vibrationally. Whatever beliefs you have, your subconscious mind takes as orders to fill.

Vision Tools for Overcoming Inhibitors and Enhancing Your Beliefs

×   To expand your vision, you must engage your imagination.

×   Use your imagination by daydreaming and fantasizing.

×   Unfurl your potential by *imagining* that your dreams and fantasies are coming true. When you feel positive emotions, your subconscious believes them.

×   Remember that desires, fantasies, and dreams have a purpose—to guide you to an optimal experience that allows you to live your true life purpose.

× Understand that *unlimited thinking steps you out of ordinary reality so you can expand your vision* of what you believe is possible for you to do.

× Use your imagination to step out of the past experiences that created your limited beliefs.

× Think in terms of possibilities.

× Command your subconscious mind to assist you in attracting and creating your vision.

× When fantasizing:

　× Think of *many* desirable outcomes.

　× Ask yourself, "What is the best possible outcome?"

　× Nudge yourself to imagine something even greater.

　× More than thinking big, fantasizing is thinking *creatively*.

× Understand that the emotions behind your thoughts have an impact on the speed with which what you are focused on will manifest. More feel-good emotions equals faster manifestation. Thoughts and beliefs aligned with your desires create feel-good emotions.

× Most people think that having (what they want) will fill a need and allow them to experience *something* that they don't have now. This *something* is always associated with a feeling, such as power, aliveness, well-being, peace, security, the ability to relax, freedom from worry, and so forth. For example, having a friend might really mean feeling companionship. Having a boss that you like might really mean feeling appreciated. Having a team that works well might really mean feeling secure in your job because your boss is pleased with your leadership.

× Reverse the process to magnetize the essence of what you want to feel. Look at your wish list. Now use imagery or fantasy to create the feelings you want from the relationship wish lists you identified in step two, in Chapter 6. Whatever you think a particular relationship will do for you—such as give you peace of mind, freedom, self-esteem, companionship, security, love, respect, and so forth—*it needs to be created within you* to make you more magnetically aligned to attract the relationship.

× View relationships as *a way to help both of you express yourselves and to create your dreams*, rather than viewing the other person and the relationship as something that will fill a void or a need.

× Take a moment and ask yourself: What do you think having this relationship, or some aspect of this relationship, will give you that you don't have now? You might want more appreciation and respect from your boss—what deep desire would feel satisfied if you had this wish fulfilled?

× Some people think that having a new relationship, or changing some aspect of a current relationship, will enable them to feel secure, safe, loved, or some other desired feeling. This is only a temporary feeling. Security, safety, love, respect, and so forth must come from within before they are experienced externally.

× Once you have identified the deeper desires you think a relationship will fulfill, you can *start fulfilling those desires now without waiting for the relationship to show up*.

× *Should*, *must*, and *ought to* statements do not give us positive emotion to help us attract our relationship desires. They indicate judgment and create negative emotion. Substitute *can*, *will*, and *choose to* statements that inspire positive emotions of possibility.

× Focus on the feelings of satisfaction, peace, joy, or well-being associated with attracting your desires to align your consciousness with the pleasure of elevated belief.

BUILD YOUR STAIRCASE

An important part of activating your intentions in step three is to build your staircase (see Figure 7-1 on the next page) to achieve your relationship goals. Whatever we want in life comes to us through the relationships we build with other people. For every relationship goal you have set, there are other people who are seeking to have a relationship with you to fulfill their relationship goals. As you are looking for them, they are looking for you. Building your staircase, therefore, means mapping out how you are going to get to your bigger relationship goals. You build your staircase by creating objectives and strategies to help you reach each goal leading to your vision.

Define the first steps on your staircase by asking yourself, *What do I believe is achievable?* Break down your vision until you have identified some initial smaller goals that you believe you can achieve and that you can put your full passion behind.

First, let's define some of the terms used on the staircase diagram in Figure 7-1.

Definitions of Terms

Mission: Your basic purpose in life and reason for being.

Vision: How you are going to live out your mission in a broad way. Where you see yourself in a specific period of time. For example, you may have a vision of your life five years from now.

Goals: What you are reaching for to help you achieve your broader vision.

Objectives: What you want to accomplish through achieving the goal. There may be more than one objective for each goal.

Strategies: The tasks you do to accomplish your objectives and to move toward your goal.

Intention: A strong desire coupled with a strong belief.

Figure 7-1
Activate Your Intentions

YOUR VISION

Activate your intentions by building a staircase of believable goals, attainable objectives, and doable strategies that leads from your wish list to your vision (where you want to be). Awareness of your mission (or sense of purpose) creates a strong foundation upon which to build your staircase. It is often easier to meet smaller goals and achieve smaller successes before you move up the stairs to face your larger goals and greater work.

Goal #4
Objectives & Strategies

Goal #3
Objectives & Strategies

Goal #2
Objectives & Strategies

Goal #1
Objectives & Strategies

Wish List

YOUR MISSION
(Life Purpose)

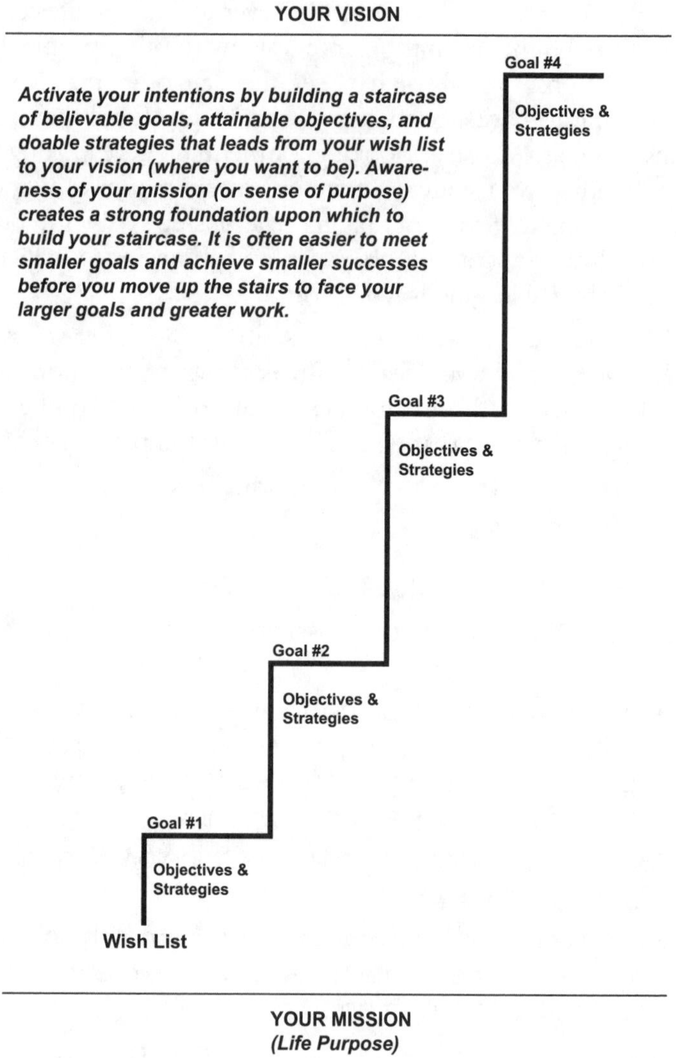

Let me give an example from my own life. My mission statement is *inspiring purposeful, passionate, and joyous living*.

My Vision is to *cultivate a strong sense of well-being in the general public*.

I set a goal to educate people on how unresolved issues in relationships impact our health and well-being.

One of the objectives that came out of this goal was to publish articles about relationships and health on highly visible Websites.

I had three strategies for achieving my goal to educate people:

1. Contact the editors of major health Websites to see if they were open to the idea of my writing for them.

2. Get their submission criteria for Web articles.

3. Write and submit my articles.

By taking action on each of the strategy steps I listed, I was fulfilling my mission, vision, and major goal. My articles were published. From the responses of readers, I could see the positive impact I was having by accomplishing my goal.

Individuals do not necessarily have to determine their life purpose or have a formal vision statement to use the four-step Harmonic Matching Process. What is more important is to have a sense of what you as an individual or as an organization want to achieve in three, five, or 10 years. Often a clearer vision will emerge from using the Harmonic Matching Process.

The most important characteristics for creating a vision statement are that it:

× Consists of broad but meaningful statements.

× Inspires passion.

× Is in alignment with the mission or purpose of the individual or organization.

× Is measurable or verifiable in the defined timeframe.

You can use the Harmonic Matching Process to discover your purpose, your vision, and your life's work. What is important for employees is to find alignment between their individual goals and those of the organization they work for. This alignment is the key to engaging employees with purpose and passion. Commitment to an organization stems from individuals knowing how they fit in to the bigger picture. It comes from believing in what you are doing and knowing that you are having a positive impact in a way that you have defined as meaningful. It comes from knowing desirable options are available to you, that you are someone who creates your future rather than allowing things to happen to you. Purpose and passion stem from individuals who can follow the lead of others they trust, and can also be leaders when opportunity knocks. Individuals who live and work purposefully and passionately take responsibility for their decisions, positive or negative, by learning from every experience, rather than seeing others (particularly their employer) as the source of their well-being.

DISCOVER YOUR LIFE'S WORK

The first principle of ethical power is Purpose. By purpose, I don't mean your objective or intention—something toward which you are always striving. Purpose is something bigger. It is the picture you have of yourself—the kind of person you want to be or the kind of life you want to lead.

—Ken Blanchard

Most of us want to feel that we have a purpose for existing. I don't mean your daily schedule or to-do list. I mean something that you feel passionate about accomplishing and leaving behind after you are no longer living. We more easily transcend those challenging days at home and in the office when we have a burning desire to do something.

How do you determine your real purpose in life? Here are some clues you may receive regarding your true life's mission:

×   Your life purpose is revealed through your feelings, imagination, desires, fantasies, and dreams.

×   You are guided to your life's work by tuning in to what feels good.

×   Your life's work is something you naturally think about, feel connected to, are familiar with, or are already doing.

×   It may be something you do for enjoyment in your free time.

×   It may be something you tell yourself you would like to do if you had more time or money or more of some other resource.

×   Your life's work may not exist as a job you will find. It could be a job you will create.

×   You may not have to make a dramatic shift in order to do your life's work. What you are doing now is often the basis of your life's work.

Next, start working toward achieving your life's purpose:

×   Respect and honor your deepest desires, for they are messages from your true self about the life you came to live.

×   Know the essence of what you want by asking, What purpose will it serve?

×   Revise your wish lists to make them as specific as you can.

×   Start creating your list of goals. Take what is not working for you and state the opposite. Transform the negative into the positive.

×   Ask yourself, What feeling am I looking for in my work? For example:

   ×   Aliveness

   ×   Excitement

   ×   Passion

- × Freedom
- × Joy
- × Abundance
- × Well-being
- × Prosperity

× Ask yourself, How can I experience these feelings or qualities now?

× What other things or situations might provide the essence of what you want?

× Set the intention to recognize opportunities aligned with your life's work.

× Set the intention to feel more joy. As you do so, you will be aligned with opportunities to be fulfilled and to be living your life's purpose.

It is helpful to understand how to write intentions to enhance the command you are giving to your subconscious. Following are some guidelines to assist you with creating powerful intention statements.

Guidelines for Writing Intentions

× Write in the present tense. Write "I have a great boss," not "I will have a great boss."

× Keep a positive focus. Give attention to what you desire rather than the lack of anything. Write "I work with a highly committed team," rather than "The individuals in my department need to have more commitment."

× Keep your statements personal. Write about yourself or your relationship with others. Refrain from comparing yourself to others.

× Use words that generate positive emotion. Write "I'm *ecstatic* about this new opportunity at work," rather than "I hope I don't have to work late to complete this project."

×   Make your intentions believable. The stronger your belief is, the more powerful your subconscious is in helping you attract your desires.

×   Be ideal-oriented. Focus on achieving your goal. Write "Our project is going smoothly and everything is working out for the best," rather than "Our project is up and down. I sure hope we can make it work!"

×   Be results-oriented. Focus on the end result rather than the process. Write "I met a great friend," rather than "I met a new friend while playing tennis."

×   Maintain the highest degree of integrity. Focus on what you desire instead of what others want for you or what you think you "should" want. Routinely set intentions for higher levels of joy in all areas of your life.

Remember that an intention is defined as strong desire coupled with strong belief. The lists of intentions must be believable to you for your subconscious to align with them and create what you are stating you want. If they are not believable, then rewrite them so that you are in alignment. Otherwise, you will be mis-creating.

INTENTIONS, PLANS, ALIGNMENT

Activating your intentions is a heart-centered exercise integrated with an intellectual planning process. The main reason for creating your staircase is to elevate and focus your belief that you can reach your goals. When you align your most passionate feel-good emotions with specific desires and create goals and objectives and strategies you can believe in, then you have *activated* your intentions.

Activated intentions command your subconscious to manifest your desires as realities in your life. The combination of good feelings with strong beliefs about goals you feel passionate about creates a magnetic energy within your vibrational consciousness. You start seeing opportunities and relationships that are aligned with your goals everywhere.

You may attract a relationship that lifts you to new heights more quickly than you might have believed possible. New options and opportunities that you had not considered before present themselves to you. Your goals evolve as you discover these new options and new forms of support. You do not necessarily have to climb every step by yourself. You may choose to take an elevator to a higher part of your staircase. You may redesign your staircase as you climb and discover new desires and new possibilities.

It is important to approach the process of transforming your life in a spirit of lightheartedness. Have fun with it. Explore and experiment with options even as you keep your focus on what you really love. When you hold the energy of your activated intentions with joy, you have room for the creative flow that can take you to outcomes that are even better than you imagined.

The way I help organizational leaders engage and empower people with purpose and passion is through the four-step Harmonic Matching Process. When people use this process to activate their intentions and build their staircases, they will be doing their jobs with purpose and passion.

TRANSFORMATIONAL BOOSTERS

Activate your intentions with these transformational boosters:

×   Remember that the closer your intentions are to your true life purpose, the more passionate you will feel about achieving them. Get to the essence of your desired goals by asking what feelings you are seeking. The essence of a new boss, for example, may translate into "someone who appreciates me." When you discover the essence of what you really want and look for ways to create those feelings now, you will strengthen your ability to activate your intentions.

× Use believable imagery to create the feelings you are seeking *right now*. Because your subconscious does not know you are creating imagery, it will assume what you are imagining is real and interpret this as a command to help you attract more of the same. This aligns you harmonically with the relationships and opportunities you want.

× Investigate how your habitual coping mechanisms and conditioned inhibitors generate limiting beliefs. Recognize that you have the power to change your beliefs into more positive ones that help you reach your goals.

× Create your staircase showing the steps you intend to take to reach your vision. Each step consists of a goal, at least one objective, and usually several strategies.

× Look at your most desired goals and think about how strongly you believe you can achieve them. Choose to work toward the goals that are the most believable. After you have had some success, move toward more challenging goals.

× Visualize the process you will go through to achieve the objectives and strategies that will bring you to your goal. Bring good feelings and positive beliefs into each small part of the process, especially if you notice a step that brings up resistance, fears, or any negative emotion. Adjust the process until you feel good about all the steps. Remember to enjoy the journey, not just the finish line.

× Think about your personal goals and be sure they are what you really want, not what someone else has told you to want. Look for ways to align your goals more precisely with your life's purpose. Creating a vibrational consciousness that is aligned with your desires rather than your fears strengthens your attracting power.

× Elevate your self-worth. Your level of self-worth is the launching pad from which you attract and create desires. If your value is based on something external, such as how someone feels about you, then you are standing on a weak platform and are positioned to mis-create. Learn to enjoy the process of getting to know yourself better. Be gentle with yourself. Remember that self-criticism is a form of self-sabotage. Learn from your experiences. Self-awareness and compassion help you elevate your vibrational consciousness to be in alignment with your desires.

× Relax and encourage yourself to be lighthearted about the process. Create your vision and staircase as an adventure rather than a homework assignment. Have fun with the process. Lightheartedness enhances well-being.

At-a-Glance Reference Guide for Step Three of the Harmonic Process

Review this summary of what you learned in step three about activating your intentions.

× Step three tells how to transform wishes and affirmations into activated intentions by aligning strong desire with strong belief.

× When you become more self-aware and understand your defense mechanisms, you open your mind and your heart to realizing your life's purpose and aligning with passion and purpose.

× When you explore your coping mechanisms, you learn how to find healthier ways of meeting your underlying needs and keeping them from becoming barriers to achieving what you want in life.

✗ Learn this fundamental principle: The beliefs you hold in your subconscious about yourself, others, situations, and circumstances are attracted again and again through all of your experiences in your life. Learn also that you can change those beliefs.

✗ Stop mis-creating your life. When you allow negative conditioned patterns such as belief in scarcity in your subconscious to attract negative circumstances into your life, you are mis-creating and becoming a victim. For example, when you say, "I want to be promoted, but they'll never see me as a leader," you are seeing yourself as a victim. You can shift your thoughts. Instead, say, "I will obtain the necessary skills and obtain a leadership role in this organization or elsewhere."

✗ Become more aware of your self-talk. Choose to use positive language. Make believable statements about yourself and your ability to achieve your goals.

✗ If you are not feeling a strong belief that you can achieve your vision or your big goals, step back and work toward more believable goals. When you are successful, it is time to move toward more challenging goals.

✗ When we learn from undesirable experience, we get closer to achieving our desires.

✗ By discovering limiting beliefs that act as inhibitors, you can transform them into positive beliefs. You can choose to change your mind to believe that you *can* have what you want. Set an intention to align with the belief system necessary to create a particular desire.

✗ Use imagery or fantasy to creatively visualize your desires as though they were already present in your life. Doing this will enhance your beliefs and strengthen your attracting power.

×   Build your staircase, which is a map of how you are going to attain the relationships and opportunities you want. The staircase shows you how to step up to your vision by creating goals, objectives, and strategies. Small, achievable tasks help you move toward your bigger goal or your vision.

×   Discover your true life's work and purpose by tuning in to what feels good to you. Your life's purpose is revealed through your feelings, imagination, desires, fantasies, and dreams. Your life's work is something you naturally think about, feel connected to, are familiar with, or are already doing.

×   Activate your intentions by aligning your feel-good emotions with specific desired goals you believe you can achieve. This creates a powerful vibrational consciousness that attracts opportunities and relationships to your life.

×   Use the Harmonic Matching Process to inspire yourself to achieve purposeful, passionate, and joyous living. Both individuals and organizations can use the process.

Now that you have learned the many ways to activate your intentions, it is time to move on to the last crucial step to fulfilling relationship intentions. In step four, explained in the next chapter, you will learn the importance of releasing the outcome of every situation.

CHAPTER EIGHT

STEP FOUR:
Release the Outcome

The base of the work is one of individuals believing in themselves, trusting themselves in the moment and being accepting of themselves and the people around them.... Once you're in play, you're in the moment. You're not judgmental, you're enjoying each other, you're accepting of everything that goes on; you're trusting yourself and just doing the game as best as you can. Your critical mind is gone, your analytical mind is not involved. Really, it's just the flow that goes on between human beings....

—Martin de Maat

The point of step four: releasing outcomes means letting go of resistance.

Like an arrow released and speeding toward the target, releasing the outcome allows your intentions to be fulfilled. In step three, you learned to activate your intentions, which might be compared to aiming the arrow and pulling back the bowstring to give the arrow the power to fly. Until your metaphorical arrow is released in step four, however, there can be no fulfillment of your desired goals.

HOLDING ON INHIBITS SUCCESS

If your peace of mind or your happiness is on hold as you wait for something to show up, then what you are waiting for will never show up...and you will keep waiting until you finally decide to let go. Until you let go, you are like an archer who cannot release the bowstring. However far the bow is bent, however carefully the shot is aimed, nothing happens until she releases the bowstring and the arrow flies toward the target.

BARRIERS AND RESISTANCE

Your negative emotions create barriers and resistance to achieving your desired goals. There are three major inhibitors to letting go and releasing your intentions:

1. Fear.
2. Judgment.
3. Feelings of inadequacy.

No matter how many affirmations you speak, these three major barriers can prevent you from achieving success. You must learn to release them and allow your intentions to be fulfilled. After you have activated your intentions, let them go. Live in the present. Get on with your life and know that your desires will show up at the perfect time and in the perfect way. Look forward with pleasure to what you are creating. Wrap good thoughts and feelings around all your desires, then let go and get on with your life.

Release Fear; Replace It With Trust

Release fear by setting the intention to trust in your ability to manifest your highest good.

Do you remember the popular acronym, FEAR? It means False Evidence Appearing Real. The false evidence comes from old, conditioned patterns in our minds. It appears real to us until we make a decision to let go and trust that we can manifest our desires.

Let's look at some key points about how fear works:

× The stronger the desire, the bigger the fear that we will not be able to receive what we want.

× The more attention we give to our fears, the less chance we have of attracting what we desire.

× Fear can arise because of conditioning from past experiences.

× Fear stems from lack of belief that we can have what we desire. Fear comes from:

    × Lack of understanding how to be a deliberate creator.

    × Lack of understanding that we can transcend undesirable situations.

    × Lack of faith that we can create new desirable realities.

Replacing fear with trust allows your intentions to move freely toward your desired outcomes.

Release Judgment; Replace It With Allowing

Release judgment by setting a clear intention to let go of thoughts that do not serve you.

When we project judgment onto others, we give away our own power. When we put emotional energy into judging someone, we attract the very thing we are rejecting because we are giving it energy.

Why would you want to give your power to something you do not like? If you become resentful toward someone for something he has done, you give him power over you. No one can make you feel anything, and you cannot make anyone feel something. We alone are responsible for our feelings and actions. No matter what happens, you have the freedom to *choose* how you will feel and respond to any outside stimulus.

Here are some points about how judgment works:

×   Blaming others for your reality takes away your belief in your own power.

×   Focusing energy on what you do not like attracts it to you.

×   Judging creates resistance to what you want.

×   Elevating your consciousness to forgiveness and compassion fills your vibrational space with positive energy. Negative energies cannot occupy the same space with positive vibrational consciousness.

×   Setting intentions to feel good allows negative energy to roll off you and flow away. Your subconscious will assist you once you are clear in your intent. Whatever comes, let it come. Whatever goes, let it go. Sustain confidence in your own power to maintain a positive creative energy.

×   Choosing to be a deliberate creator of your own experience leads to success. Do not think you are a victim of anything or anyone outside of you.

×   Blaming yourself produces no beneficial outcomes and creates barriers to taking positive action.

Releasing judgment, against yourself or others, removes resistance to having what you want.

Release Feelings of Inadequacy; Replace Them With Self-Esteem

Positive self-esteem is essential to creating positive outcomes for any desire. Here are some points about releasing feelings of inadequacy and enhancing your self-esteem:

×   You can choose to be an optimist. This is a conscious choice you can turn into a habit.

x When self-esteem is strong, we believe we have desirable options.

x Our level of self-worth impacts our degree of belief that we can have what we want.

x Until you learn to love yourself, it is difficult to love anyone else.

x True self-esteem is actually the opposite of arrogance or conceited egotism. Self-esteem is relaxed and confident, whereas egotism is an artificial coping mechanism developed to cover lack of self-esteem.

x Respect yourself by showing up for yourself. Take the time to develop deeper self-understanding and self-knowledge. Be gentle with yourself.

x Have compassion for yourself in undesirable situations. Give yourself a break and let go of blaming yourself or anyone else.

x Change the way you talk about yourself, both out loud to others and in your head to yourself. Switch from negative to positive words and phrases.

x Learn from every experience that strengthens your confidence and self-esteem.

x Align yourself with a consciousness of abundance. Start by seeing what you already have as an example of abundance. This automatically attracts more abundance.

x Spend time each day being nice to yourself by doing things that bring you pleasure.

x Decide to identify with the creator role and let the victim role go. Become a conscious and deliberate creator of positive thoughts, feelings, beliefs, and outcomes.

× Take the time to listen to yourself and discover your heart's desire. Be true to yourself and stand up for your dreams.

× Build your self-esteem by listing your positive qualities and achievements.

Releasing feelings of inadequacy and replacing them with feelings of self-esteem allows your positive vibrational consciousness to attract the outcomes you want into your life.

Some years ago, I was taking a water aerobics class as part of my orientation to well-being. It was a wonderful class, and I really loved it. The instructor was very inspiring, and there were some truly beautiful people there. Water aerobics was something I did to feel good and take better care of myself. When we all jumped in the water, everyone just naturally fell into their places.

Somehow I kept winding up next to a woman who complained the whole time about the music, the temperature, everything. It was quite disturbing to my desire for peace. How did I attract this? No matter where I moved in the pool, that woman seemed to find a place right beside me. All she did was complain, and I was allowing her negativity to ruin my wonderful class.

After several days of being irritated and feeling my energy falling, I decided not to focus on how I attracted this woman and her complaints but to give attention to how I wanted the experience to be. I wanted to be with people who were really into the class, who enjoyed the experience, and who were quiet. I realized that this woman obviously had some issues, so I focused on sending her good thoughts and feeling compassion. I consciously decided to release my irritation with her. I just mapped out in my mind how I wanted the class to be for me and held that vision. The very next day, instead of coming to where I was standing, the complaining woman went to the far end of the pool!

Now this was a pretty powerful demonstration to me. Before, she had found me wherever I moved. But now I had decided that I would not be affected by her. I would stay in a higher vibrational consciousness. I felt compassion for her, but I understood that her issues had nothing to do with me. When I had been irritated, she had stuck to me like glue. No matter what I tried, I could not get away from her. And then...when I shifted my consciousness, she just moved away.

We need to hold the vision of how we want our experience to be. If we think our well-being depends on what any other person does, we set ourselves up for failure. It is not about expecting someone else to change. It is about holding a vision in our mind and in our heart of what we want.

Timing, Dominant Intention, Dominant Vibration

Your dominant intention is the focus of what you *say*; your expressed intention. Your dominant intention overrides all other intentions when intentions contradict one another.

Your dominant or prevailing vibration is what you *believe* and project from your conscious and subconscious mind. This is what magnetizes our experiences. It is determined by the combined frequency of our thoughts, feelings, and beliefs about a particular desire.

Letting go and releasing the outcome means trusting in your ability to draw from the stream of life what you need and want at just the right time. The more all of your intentions are lined up in an integrated vision of your life purpose, and aligned with the highest good for all, the more powerful they are when they are released. Set positive intentions, then let go and trust that they will arrive on the right schedule.

In my 20s, I wanted to get my MBA, so I started looking into programs. I wanted to get into a top MBA program for executives returning to school so I could study with other older executives. I set my intention to get the most I could out of the experience. But the cost of every program was prohibitive for me.

I refused to give up. I looked at the brochure regularly and put it up on my bulletin board at work. There were no scholarships or grants for the program, so I began holding the vision that someone would pay for it. Despite the intensity of my intention, however, my fear was in the way. When I got a new job, I inquired, but there was still no money for my MBA.

At that point, I let it go. It was as though I gave up. But I was not really giving up because I was not depressed or down about it. I just stopped putting my peace of mind on hold. I was letting go of being on hold. Although I still wanted the MBA from that program, I knew I could live without it. This was not something I needed to get where I was going in life. With or without it, I would create my life goals. This was my way of releasing the outcome.

A few years later, another company called to recruit me for a new position. Even though I loved the job I was in at that time, I said, "I'll come if you'll pay for my MBA." The recruiting executive said they would. I promptly gave notice to my employer. Now, here came my opportunity.

But a few days later I got a follow-up call. "I'm sorry," the recruiter said. "I made a promise I shouldn't have made. We don't have the funds for your MBA program." So there I was. I had given notice. I was leaving a job I loved. Still no MBA. And then, as I was sitting there thinking about the call, the president of the hospital where I worked came into my office. "Margaret," she said, "we're not going to let you leave. We are going to pay for your MBA degree."

What I realized was that when I had first expressed my interest in getting an MBA, I had also set the intention to get the maximum out of the program. I had a strong intention to do well in it; that was my dominant vibration. As it turned out, I was a much more seasoned executive at age 34, when I got it, than I had been at age 29, when I had initially released the intention. I needed to be lined up and ready for it. As a result, I did get a lot more out of it than I would have earlier.

When you understand how dominant vibration works, you can see how your subconscious mind supports you in attracting your highest intention. Things that the conscious mind sees as barriers are not barriers to the subconscious. If we are completely clear when we release our intention, we just *know*. That's the way our mind works. The result may come in a different way and in a different time than we expected. We need to trust that life will bring it to us. When we have no trust, fear comes in and inhibits the process.

Activate your intentions and goals. Create your vision board and your staircase. Then put them away. Don't keep staring at them past the point where they make you feel good. If you don't let go, if you keep hanging on, you are continually reminded that you have not yet met your goal. If you start feeling bad about your situation, let go and put it in a drawer. What you want will arrive when the timing is right. Refer to Figure 8-1 to further your understanding of timing with regard to manifestation.

Figure 8-1
Impact of Inhibitors* on the
Timing of Manifestation

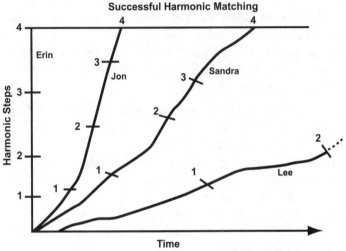

Erin	Zero resistance in each harmonic step resulting in instantaneous manifestation.	
Jon	Minor Resistance in each harmonic step resulting in some time delay in manifesation.	
Sandra	Moderate Resistance in each harmonic step resulting in a moderate time delay in manifestation.	
Lee	Great Resistance in each harmonic step resulting in a great time delay in manifestation.	

Inhibitors = Resistance: What We Criticize, Justify, Fear, Worry About, Defend Against, Prepare Against or Struggle With

WHAT YOU RESIST — YOU ATTRACT!!

LETTING GO BRINGS POSITIVE OUTCOMES

Letting go allows your activated intentions to go forth and be fulfilled. You will want to create a vibrational consciousness to support the process of releasing the outcome of your intentions, including:

× Trust and Belief.

× Relax and Release.

× Allowing.

× Gratitude.

× Forgiveness.

× Integrity and Wholeness.

× Self-Love/Self-Esteem.

× Optimism.

Let's look at how each of these positive qualities helps you to release the outcome.

Trust and Belief

As you develop greater trust that life is a flowing, creative process and that you have the ability to make positive choices, you will find it easier to release your intentions. The stronger your belief in your own ability to participate creatively in life, the easier it becomes for you to release outcomes. You can always create new goals and intentions as you move forward and see more options. No situation is an all-or-nothing deal. Life is alive and full of possibilities. We always have choices. We have a quiver full of arrows. If one arrow does not hit the target, or if you see a better target, you can always shoot another arrow.

Develop trust by strengthening both your determination to be a conscious creator and your belief that you have that ability to make choices. For a deliberate creator, life is not static; life is recognized as a constantly moving stream of change that can be directed by the energy of your vibrational consciousness. The strength of this true belief allows you to be more adventurous and more playful, which opens up more opportunities.

Trust life and allow yourself to be alive. Living things grow.

Relax and Release

Whereas relaxation allows us to let go and release outcomes, tension constricts the flow of energy and keeps us stuck. When we are coming from fear, we automatically tighten up. Constriction makes us think we have no choice and that we just have to accept the situation we are in. Fear may cause us to think in black and white terms: Either we must do something drastic or something terrible will happen.

The more you can relax, even in difficult circumstances, the more you will see that there are many choices available. Relaxing allows you to be open to new possibilities and see many options. When you release the outcome of your intention in a relaxed way, you send a positive message to your subconscious that directs it to attract what you want in ways that are truly for your highest good. If you try to release the outcome, but you are still holding on to a restricted idea of how the outcome should manifest, you limit the possibilities. Relax and allow a positive focus on well-being to attract the best outcome for all.

Allowing

Allowing is different from tolerating. Allowing does not mean you have to put up with someone or something. Allowing creates a positive emotional state because it is not resisting the way life is. Life permits everyone to make both positive and negative choices. When you come from a place of allowing, you are thus giving yourself the freedom to choose to attract positive outcomes into your life.

Tolerating a situation we do not like creates negative emotions and beliefs. When we are coming from a place of putting up with a negative situation or relationship, we are telling our subconscious that we believe that we have no other choice.

People often try to create meaning in their lives (consciously or unconsciously) by identifying with the victim role. By blaming someone else for our troubles, we can claim an excuse for not making the effort to try to have a satisfying life. But who really wants to live like that? You do have a choice.

Here are some things to consider that will raise your vibrational consciousness:

×   Allow yourself to feel what you feel and to learn which thoughts and beliefs created your feelings.

×   Allow yourself to remain calm and to avoid creating negative dramas.

×   Allow yourself to believe that any situation can be changed for the better.

×   Allow the possibility of new opportunities, new options, and new relationships.

×   Allow your beliefs to become increasingly more positive.

×   Allow life to bring you what you want. When you release outcomes in a spirit of allowing, you open the door to seemingly miraculous results. This is because you are not restricting the subconscious from finding the best path to your highest good.

Gratitude

Nothing attracts positive outcomes more powerfully than gratitude. When you allow yourself to feel grateful for every little good thing in your life, you fill up with good feelings and elevate your vibrational consciousness to the highest level.

Gratitude sends a strong emotional message to your subconscious: "Bring more good things into my life!" Allow yourself to feel glad and be thankful for as many things as you can think of. This is easy to do and can be enormously pleasant to do. Here are some suggestions for affirmations of gratitude.

I am grateful:

×   That I am learning how to attract positive relationships and situations.

×   That I am learning to make conscious choices and to release what no longer serves me.

×   For all the people and situations that brought me to this point in my life.

×   To myself for surviving all the challenges that I have experienced and for all the strength I learned from every difficulty that brought me to this point.

×   For all the simple pleasures of life and for being able to feel them.

×   To myself for having the self-respect to make a decision to shift toward creating positive thoughts, emotions, beliefs, and goals.

×   For every dream I have for attracting good relationships and opportunities.

×   For being alive and knowing that life allows change.

Release the outcome of your intentions in a spirit of gratitude.

Forgiveness

I define forgiveness as a head and heart decision to move forward by ceasing to judge ourselves or others. By forgiving, we release the negative thoughts and emotions associated with a situation or person. We know when we have truly forgiven ourselves or others because we feel lighter and happier, and we have new energy to start a new project, clean our houses, or clear out the old stuff we've been storing in our attics or basements. When we forgive, we are clearing out the stuff in our heads and in our hearts that no longer serves us. This naturally results in a strong desire to clear out the space around us.

Judgment usually occurs when we experience hurt or anger. (Anger is a secondary emotion stemming from hurt.) These emotions crop up under various circumstances, including misunderstandings or when we think someone has betrayed us, offended us, lied to us, or rejected us. In the workplace, forgiveness is called for with regularity. It is easy to step on each others' toes when working on tight deadlines and intense projects. When you are passed by for a promotion or if you are denied the bonus you were hoping for, then it is necessary to forgive in order to free your energy and continue doing your best work. In our personal lives, if we have unresolved hurt it can impact our home life as well as our productivity at work.

Forgiveness allows you to release the outcome of your intentions cleanly. Forgiveness frees you from old baggage. Spend as much time as you have to, but come to forgiveness. Release old patterns and be free to attract new possibilities.

Integrity and Wholeness

Integrity means being honest with and true to yourself. Because *integrity* and *integrated* are related words, its other meaning is being whole. When you are integrated, it is easy to release the outcome of your intentions because you have full faith in the truth of your intentions.

If you are having difficulty releasing the outcome of an intention, sometimes the reason is that a part of you is not convinced that you really want what you are saying you want. When you are feeling uncomfortable about releasing an intention, it is a good idea to review it and check to see if you are 100 percent behind it. You may be able to shift an inner resistance if your goal truly is something you want. If the resistance is more substantial, however, it does no good to try to force yourself to believe in it. You may have to go back and refine the intention until it matches harmonically with what you truly desire. Otherwise, you will not be coming from integrity.

Wholeness is also closely connected with well-being. When all your desired goals for the different relationships in your personal and professional life fit together into an integrated vision, you will be coming from wholeness. The more all of your goals and intentions are congruent with what you truly want and with your life purpose, the more smoothly you will be able to release them.

When you have integrity in your purpose, you can more easily trust that life will fulfill what you have called for. It becomes easy to set intentions and let them go into the stream of life. What else would you do other than allow your dreams to unfold into your life's purpose? That is what you do.

Wholeness gives you a naturally focused passion that can also be lighthearted and relaxed. This emphasizes the importance of setting your intentions for the highest good of all concerned. When you take into consideration the whole system of relationships you are connected to, you increase your own inner wholeness, and life creates less resistance to bringing your intentions to reality.

Self-Love/Self-Esteem

To build self-love and self-esteem, bring feel-good moments, memories, and fantasies into your thoughts as often as possible. Make a habit of being nice to yourself. Show compassion for yourself. Get into the habit of enjoying your daydreams and visions of what you like, want, and desire. Experience loving yourself as a deep feeling of inner joy and well-being. True joy is never found through anyone or anything outside you. What you experience outside is a reflection of your inner sense of well-being.

Even if you feel pretty good about yourself, decide to love yourself better. Get to know yourself better. Become your own best friend. You are the only person that you will spend all of your life with, so you might as well be friendly with you. Go deep within and replace fears, judgments, and feelings of inadequacy with love. This is the state that allows you to completely release the outcome of your intentions. When you are full of love, you can set a strong intention and let it go freely into the stream of life.

Truly loving yourself fills you up and gives you love to share with others. This state is playful and lighthearted. It allows you to co-create with others easily and makes you receptive to the new relationships and opportunities it attracts.

Optimism

Decide to be an optimist. A person who is optimistic learns from undesirable circumstances rather than getting caught up in the blame game. The optimistic viewpoint gathers the most value from every experience and anticipates positive outcomes in the future. It is an attitude that attracts vitality because optimism is unshakably focused on belief in possibility—belief that all things are possible and that you can have what you want. Just remember that dominant vibration prevails. For instance, if you set an intention to have a strong, productive, and cohesive team at work and you also want to hire a specific individual who applied for a vacant position, these two intentions may not both be met if the prospective employee is not in alignment with your dominant or prevailing vibration.

Release the outcome of your intentions in the spirit of optimism and trust in your well-being. Well-being is felt at greater levels when you learn to set intentions and when you let go for your highest good and the highest good of all concerned.

Surrender Circumstances That No Longer Serve

When you are in the process of creating and setting positive goals for what you want, your vibrational consciousness becomes higher and you may find that some of the circumstances, people, or situations in your life are no longer in alignment with your intentions. As your thoughts, emotions, and beliefs shift into more positive vibrational energy, circumstances that are not in harmony with your consciousness will simply no longer fit into your life.

As you are shifting energies, you may experience what feels like a period of chaos, as you are in the middle of a tug of war between the conflicting beliefs you still hold in your subconscious and your conscious intentions. At some point in the process of setting intentions for how you want to experience each segment of your day, you will find that you naturally let go of what no longer serves you. Only what is in resonance remains. This means anyone or anything that is not a harmonic match with your dominant vibration will automatically drop out of your experience, and anyone or anything that is a match will remain. You will not be able to hold on to things that are not harmonious with the beliefs in your subconscious. Attempting to hold on will create a barrier to having what you want. This is why this fourth step of releasing the outcome is so important to the process of deliberately creating your reality.

Relationship Boundaries

It is important to establish and maintain healthy relationship boundaries. When we lack a clear sense of individual identity, people often break through or leap over our personal boundaries. We may also cross other people's boundaries. We may hold the irrational belief that *I am nobody without someone in my life* or *I am nobody without the approval or acceptance of a particular person in your life*. This kind of thinking makes us very dependent on that other person. It also makes it difficult to create an identity separate from that person. If we are in this position, we may be willing to do whatever it takes to preserve that negative relationship, including giving up health, money, security, identity, intelligence, spiritual beliefs, family, country, job, community, friends, values, honor, and (finally) all self-respect. If we wish to have our own lives and fulfill our own desires, we need to have boundaries. We must set positive intentions. Some of these intentions are explored in the following paragraphs. Remember, an intention is different from an affirmation. An intention is very personal and involves having strong belief that you can create the desire. When desire exist without significant belief then it is an affirmation. Review the sample intentions following, but make sure you create intentions that are believable to you.

Positive intention: I am my own person, and my relationships flourish and grow in a healthy manner.

Guilt sometimes leaves us feeling overly responsible for the welfare of others. But when we take this stance, we do not allow our friends, associates, or partners to accept personal responsibility, make their own choices, or live with the consequences of those choices. When you replace guilt with the intention to learn from every experience, you are shifting pessimistic thinking to the higher vibrational consciousness of optimistic thinking.

Positive intention: I accept personal responsibility for my own life. I accept the outcomes of the choices I make. I learn from every experience and apply this knowledge to the choices I make in all aspects of my life.

Sometimes we see others as helpless and needing us to fix their problems. We may also fear negative outcomes for others.

Positive intention: I am a loving person. I focus on taking care of myself rather than accepting the consequences of someone else's actions. I believe in the well-being of all people and assist others as I am inspired to do so.

The need to be needed can lead us to step out of integrity to address the needs of others, but that leaves us with nothing left to give ourselves. This is sacrificial giving, not inspired giving. It is based on a consciousness of scarcity, not on giving from the heart. Sacrificial giving creates heartaches and a sense of entrapment, whereas inspired giving, regardless of the level of intensity and extent, brings joy and a sense of freedom, and leaves the giver with more energy to give to himself as well as to others.

Positive intention: I always make decisions that support my sense of well-being and happiness.

Sometimes people get stuck in the belief that time will make a relationship better. They give more and more of themselves and wait longer and longer for something good to happen, and nothing ever happens and nothing ever improves. What holds us to this pattern are those fleeting moments when the relationship resembles what you would like it to be. This is called "intermittent reinforcement." It is unsatisfactory.

Positive intention: I invest time in relationships that are aligned with my desires. I create relationships that are in the highest good for all concerned.

Another boundary issue is believing that you are the problem in the relationship. You may give up who you are and become who someone else wants you to be in an attempt to make the relationship work. It does not work.

Positive intention: I am true to myself.

Positive self-esteem is the belief that you are a valuable human being who is worthy of receiving and giving unconditional love. We always draw into our experience people who confirm what we believe about ourselves. If we want to create trustworthy and fulfilling relationships, then we must have positive self-esteem. If you do not believe in yourself, how can others believe in you? How can they trust you? If you do not respect yourself, how can others respect you?

Dealing With Negative Energies of Others

Sometimes when you are trying to shift into a more positive situation and surrender circumstances that no longer serve, you run into negative energies being emitted by other people. This is a normal occurrence; something in your former belief system has attracted the energy, and now you want to make a change, but you are dealing with people who seem to be sabotaging your efforts. Here is a 30-second strategy for refocusing on well-being.

Rather than empowering the other person by getting irritated, ask yourself, "How do I want it to be with this person?" Hold your vision of a positive relationship in your consciousness. Those who are getting in your way will not be able to remain in your space when you stay aligned with positive energy. Either they will have to shift to a higher consciousness with you, or they will have to find another place to be.

When I was running a department many years ago, three people were constantly sabotaging me. It was nothing obvious that I could deal with directly, but I could tell. There was an undercurrent. I knew they were playing games. Instead of being pulled in, however, I just asked myself, "How do I want it to be with the people in my department? How do I want them to be with me?"

By holding a positive vision, I was commanding my subconscious to attract people and relationships into my department that would be coming from integrity. I set this intention: *I intend to work with people who are honest and support me with full integrity.* In doing this, I was lining up with my well-being. When people are out of alignment with our high vibrational consciousness, they just can't stay around us. Within three months, all three individuals had found other jobs. I had not intended to force them out, because forcing would only have kept me aligned with their energy, but because they were out of resonance with my dominant vibration, they had to either fall away or shift to a higher level. We could not continue to work together in the same space when my consciousness was clearly aligned with something different from theirs.

This is how life works. We attract what we are in harmony or resonance with, which means we attract what we give attention to or what we fear. In this case, I had first attracted my worse fears. This turned out to be a great learning experience for me, a lesson I have applied in my life again and again. Setting intentions is no different from tuning to a radio station. Keep the dial where you set it and your program will come in loud and clear. If you find yourself in the kind of situation I was in, do not sink into denial. Do not pretend it is not happening. Choose to redesign the situation and see it as how you want it to be for yourself and for the highest good of all concerned. Then keep moving in a positive direction and deal with the situation from a consciousness of well-being rather than one filled with fear.

In other words, *take the high road*. If you take the low road, you will attract more of the same. You will be drawn back down into a lower vibrational consciousness. When you see the other person with compassion, you are inviting her to shift to a higher level of integrity. But every person is free to find his own way. If she is unable or unwilling to relate to you positively, either she will move to another space or you will. When change happens, do not indulge in arrogant self-congratulation. Just be happy that a more harmonious situation has arrived. Gracefully surrender the circumstances that no longer serve your present state.

Reframe Undesirable Situations

How you respond to an undesirable situation depends a great deal on the perspective from which you perceive it. Reframing means choosing a positive perspective.

If you buy an art print and take it to the frame shop, you will see that it looks different depending on the frame around it. You put a different color around it, and the picture takes on a new look. Some colors make it look beautiful, but others fall flat. In the same way, a plain or fancy frame changes what a picture looks like.

We can do the same thing with our experiences. The same set of facts will look different according to the "frame" around them. This is not about denying realities, or pretending. When you choose to reframe a situation and see from the higher perspective of well-being, you get more out of that situation:

×   You learn more from the situation.

×   You see the situation shifting for the benefit of all concerned.

×   You see yourself as having options.

×   You choose a bright frame instead of a gloomy one.

Organizational leaders are becoming increasingly aware of the importance of perception and perspective in guiding management teams toward their vision. We gain greater strength when we learn how to reframe a situation by changing our perception to one of well-being and higher vibrational consciousness.

Moving to a New Identity; Releasing Victimhood

People tend to stabilize their lives by identifying with familiar roles and identities. They sometimes become comfortable being a victim. When you learn to be a deliberate creator, however, you can no longer live in victim consciousness. You become a different person.

We often go through a period of chaos during the transition, of course, because we cannot use many of the old, familiar patterns. We soon notice that we have no room to vent and complain anymore because now we know complaining just aligns us with what we do not want. Moving out of victim consciousness can be challenging to old relationships. Maybe you always got together with Jeff and Tina to complain about various favorite annoyances. However, that was your relationship then, and now you no longer want to complain all the time. Your relationship changes and Jeff and Tina no longer recognize you.

If you hold on to a victim identity, you are attracting more reasons to be a victim. Your subconscious attracts people who will victimize you and situations in which you can play out that role. That is what you are asking it to do until you release that old identity and replace it with a new, positive, creator identity. You have to consciously choose to shift to a new identity. You have to take responsibility for creating what you want. Many people, when they were growing up, were not taught to be creative and strong. In general, we have been taught to be judgmental toward ourselves and others. This blaming orientation keeps us stuck as victims.

Let us try a quick check on where you are relative to this identity:

×   Do you feel like a victim if someone rams your car?

×   Do you feel like a victim if you get passed up for a promotion?

×   Do you feel like a victim if you have to pay alimony?

Do you want to stay in that victim consciousness, or do you want to shift out of it? If you hold on to victim consciousness, you are commanding your subconscious to attract more reasons to feel victimized.

When you shift to focus out of victimization, you move into harmonic alignment with well-being. Look at any situation. If it brings up a feeling of victim consciousness, you are not fully aligned with being a deliberate creator. If you choose to identify with victim consciousness, or with a consciousness that creates victims, you are not aligned with the highest good of all. To attract your highest good, choose to shift your identity to that of a positive creator.

Co-Create With Others From Strength and Equality

A positive creator seeks to co-create with others in a balanced way. This means respecting the integrity of the people you work with and also having the strength to respect your own boundaries. Even when there is inequality of position, a positive relationship is built on an equality of respect for the other person and a sense of our own responsibility for creating harmonious outcomes. If you are managing a team, therefore, you have the responsibility to set goals and direct the work. But this can only produce harmonious outcomes when those who report to you feel that you care about them as human beings.

Even in a parent-child relationship, which is clearly unequal in authority, children need to feel that the parent loves and respects them as individuals. The parent has the responsibility to set the rules and maintain the boundaries because children don't know what is okay and what is not. But a child is much more likely to respond positively if the parent takes time to explain the reasons for the rules and shows a desire to help him grow into more responsibility.

Strong co-creators are likewise not afraid of open dialogue with those who report to them, nor are they afraid to accept direction from someone they have chosen to report to. Those who are aligned with the consciousness of harmonious matching attract and inspire others who can co-create with them on a vibrationally balanced level where each member of the team understands the roles and responsibilities of the others.

FOSTERING CONSCIOUSNESS OF ABUNDANCE AND SUCCESS

Integrity and openness encourage the development of a consciousness of abundance and attract successful relationships and opportunities. By releasing the outcome of our intentions, we open ourselves to new and better possibilities.

Allowing Organizational Outcomes to Unfold

The vice president of a large healthcare system retained me to evaluate its psychiatric services division. She wanted to know if it was viable in her market or if the company should close the program. To do this evaluation, I needed the support of the vice president to ensure that I got good data and that nothing was withheld. Understandably, she had some concerns about her job security, since she was VP of mental health and in charge of the division in question. I talked with her at some length about the Harmonic Matching Process and showed her that allowing what was good for the organization would also be good for her. While her situation was giving her an opportunity to shine and show she was a team player by looking out for what was best for the organization, she also had to come to terms with the reality that being in integrity and offering valuable data for the analysis might cost her job. When she opened up to this possibility and released the outcome, she was able to become secure enough that her well-being no longer depended on the organization or anything else outside herself. If she held on to living in fear, it might result in the loss of her sense of integrity. She stayed open to the opportunity for something different. She was able to ask the question, "What does it mean to let go for the better good of all concerned?" In releasing the outcome, she was aligning with well-being and the highest good for the whole.

As a result of the evaluation, the company ended up keeping the program. The higher-ups realized that they had a bigger gem than they had realized. But the outcome could have been the opposite.

In another organization with a similar situation, I again worked with a vice president whose position was on the line. This individual also was able to understand the value of maintaining integrity and a positive orientation. At the end of the review process, I recommended that the hospital merge with another healthcare organization and close its psychiatric unit. Management appreciated the VP's integrity and contribution to the evaluation and worked with him to give him an extended period of time to find another position. The end result was that he found a new job that he was very happy with and which paid him more money. In addition, the new organization was closer to his home.

By coaching these two vice presidents in the Harmonic Matching Process, I was able to show them how to align with well-being and with what they really wanted, which resulted in attracting positive outcomes. I was able to coach them because I had gone through a similar situation earlier in my career when my job was being eliminated as the result of an organization-wide assessment that I had been part of. The organization needed someone with technical credentials that I did not have. I helped them with their decision to merge two internal divisions, which resulted in my position being eliminated. Although this was emotionally challenging for me, I knew I was living and working from integrity and for the best interests of the whole.

When you work with integrity and open yourself to new opportunities and better outcomes, you attract those better outcomes. When your dominant vibration is your belief that you are worthy, you will attract a good job. This is true regardless of the state of the economy. What I remind people of is this: *you just require one great job*. The state of the economy doesn't have to negatively impact you, because there is more than one great job in the world. Once you know how to harmonize your consciousness with what you desire, then you will attract it. Because all things in resonance come together, when your dominant vibration is positive, you will be able to surrender one situation and be open to receiving something that is even better. You will find a harmonic match for what you want.

AT-A-GLANCE REFERENCE GUIDE

Review this summary of what you learned in step four of the Harmonic Matching Process about releasing the outcome of your intentions and goals.

×   Step four shows you how to release the outcome of your intentions so you can attract what you want.

×   You learned that if your peace of mind or happiness is on hold as you wait for an outcome to show up, the desirable outcome will be beyond your reach.

×   When you encounter barriers and resistance caused by fear, judgment, and feelings of inadequacy, you can transform them by setting intentions to focus on trust, allowing, and self-esteem.

×   Your dominant vibration magnetizes your experiences and is determined by the combined frequency of your thoughts, beliefs, and feelings regarding a particular desire. What you attract is based on your dominant vibration, which is also referred to as your prevailing vibration.

×   If you are focused on fear of not getting what you want, that is what you will attract until you shift your vibrational consciousness to a higher level by aligning your thoughts, beliefs, and emotions with your desires.

×   When you let your intentions flow into the stream of life, your subconscious will attract what you desire in the best way and at the best time.

×   Timing (in terms of when you attract what you desire) is directly related to the degree to which you believe in your goals and release them confidently and freely. Timing is also related to what is in your highest good.

×   Positive vibrational qualities that support the release of your outcomes include trust, belief, relaxation, allowing, gratitude, forgiveness, integrity, wholeness, self-esteem, and optimism.

×   It is important to surrender and release circumstances that no longer serve your intentions.

× In discovering how to create and maintain healthy relationship boundaries, you learn how to build strong and balanced relationships.

× When dealing with negative energies from others, you learn to focus on the question, *How do I want it to be with this person?*

× By reframing undesirable situations into a more positive perspective, you become able to gain the most value and learning from every situation that comes your way.

× Being a deliberate creator does not mean blaming yourself for negative circumstances you have attracted. You attract what you are a harmonic match for. You can learn to change your vibrational consciousness. Be gentle with yourself and others as you learn.

I wish you well with your journey and implementing the Harmonic Matching Process into your life. I trust in your well-being and know that using the four-step matching process will bring greater fulfillment into your life. My clients and students continue to tell me that as they engage in the Harmonic Matching Process, their relationships are more fulfilling and their lives are richer in spirit. The best of life is before you when you treasure what you have. Thank you for allowing me to be a part of your experience by reading and absorbing the information in this book. I am eternally grateful to be doing work that I love. Imparting this information to you brings me great joy.

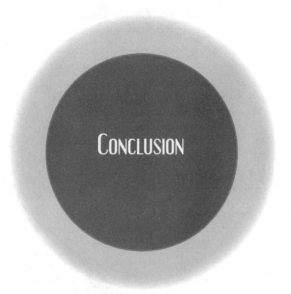

CONCLUSION

Using the Harmonic Matching Process goes beyond positive thinking and affirmations. Whatever you may be saying to yourself, it is how you *feel* about your thoughts that determines whether you will allow your desire to manifest. Successful manifestation using the four-step Harmonic Matching Process involves releasing limiting beliefs that no longer support your highest good and letting go of denser-level energies and thoughts that lower your vibratory alignment. In other words, you must choose to think about those things that bring peace and joy, delight, health, and well-being into your world.

The Harmonic Matching Process can be used much more effectively when it is consciously applied with an understanding that comes from correlating your thoughts, beliefs, and feelings with what you are attracting. Its intricacies, however, are revealed gradually as you gain mastery in using this universal law to manifest your heart's desires. Refer to Figure 8-2 to further your understanding that Harmonic Matching is an ongoing process of creating intentions and fulfilling desires.

Figure 8-2
Successful Harmonic Matching!
An Ongoing Process

Step 1: Feel Good Moments
Step 2: Identify Desires
Step 3: Activate Intentions
Step 4: Release the Outcome

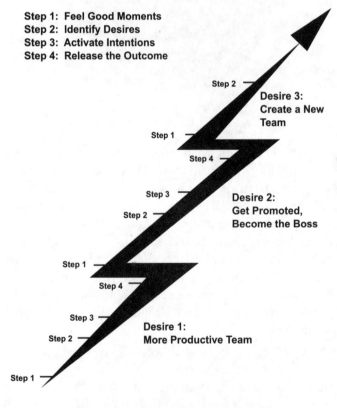

Life is a series of desires that stimulate new desires.

REVIEW OF THE HARMONIC MATCHING PROCESS

The Relationship Code shows how the Harmonic Matching Process gives you the knowledge to deliberately create a higher vibrational consciousness that attracts the relationships and opportunities you want into your life. Through this knowledge, you can engage and empower people to live and work with purpose and passion. When you have taken all four steps, you have created a vibrational consciousness that is aligned with your desires. What you focus on becomes your dominant vibration that commands your subconscious to manifest relationships and opportunities that are resonant with that vibration, and this becomes your life experience.

Step One: Create Feel-Good Moments

This step energizes your emotional resources by focusing your feelings on positive states. You learn to collect and cherish feel-good memories, dreams, and fantasies to elevate your emotions. In step one, you learn how to transform negative emotions into their opposite positive emotions. As your emotional state becomes more positive, your self-esteem increases. You learn to create positive relationships and new feel-good moments. These help you attract and inspire all of your relationships in both your personal and professional lives.

Step Two: Identify Your Desires

In this step, you learn to identify your desires and define your relationship goals by creating wish lists for different types of relationships. Step two shows us that most of what we want in life comes through relationships with other people. This step is about getting a clear idea of what you want in your personal and work relationships. When your goals are well-defined, you are guided to communicate them effectively through clear agreements. This step also emphasizes the importance of setting the intention that your goals be fulfilled for the highest good for all concerned.

Step Three: Activate Your Intentions

It is not enough to simply speak an affirmation or make a wish. This step shows how important it is to blend and align your thoughts, feelings, and beliefs to *activate* your intentions. When your intentions are activated, they become harmonically resonant with what you want. You learn how to overcome inhibitors and habitual coping mechanisms. You also learn the importance of transcending scarcity consciousness. This step shows how to elevate your beliefs and create believable goals. You learn to build your staircase to map out how you will achieve your desires and your bigger vision. Step three also shows how to discover your true life's work and your purpose. This step emphasizes the central importance of believability and of vibrational alignment of thoughts, emotions, and beliefs to engage your subconscious to manifest your desires.

Step Four: Release the Outcome

It is not enough to activate your intentions. Until you let go of the outcome, your intentions cannot flow freely into the stream of life. This step shows how releasing the outcome sends a signal to your subconscious that you are aligned with well-being and giving your intentions permission to manifest at the right time and in the right way to be aligned with your dominant vibration. When you set the intention that *this, or something better, be fulfilled for the highest good of all*, you allow your subconscious to attract the best outcomes into your life.

To Align Your Consciousness in All Four Steps, Set Your Intention...

Step 1: To feel good about where you are and about your desires.

Step 2: To be clear about what is in your best interests as you create your wish list, and to open your mind and your heart to something better, to be fulfilled for the highest good for all.

Step 3:   To be clear about lining up your consciousness with your desire by creating a staircase of goals, objectives, and strategies to align belief with desire and know you are worthy of receiving your desires.

Step 4:   To be able to release the outcome and to be peaceful and happy about what is, regardless of what is to come.

TRANSFORMATIONAL BOOSTERS

Use these boosters to help you release the outcome of your intentions:

×   Look for examples to strengthen your belief that you *can* attract what you desire. Build up the strength of your belief and *know* that it is true.

×   Be aware and notice if your peace of mind or your happiness is on hold, waiting for a desire to come to fruition. Be open-minded by setting the intention to release the expectation that your desire will be fulfilled in a specific way.

×   Choose to see the cup as half full, not half empty. Be optimistic. Be an allower. Know that you can align your consciousness to deliberately create your desires.

×   Choose to learn from experience and get the most out of what happens in your life rather than judging what you or others have attracted.

×   Be compassionate about what you or others have attracted. Be kind and gentle with yourself and others.

×   Choose to see the gifts in every situation.

×   Treasure what you have.

×   Set the intention to increase your belief that you can have what you desire. Command your subconscious to attract: *this, or something better, for the highest good*.

×   Create your staircase, action plan, and strategies to strengthen your belief. At the same time, remain open to the many possible ways your desires may be fulfilled.

×   Create passionate energy around your desire and release it to happen in the ideal way and at the ideal time.

×   Be playful and lighthearted about the process.

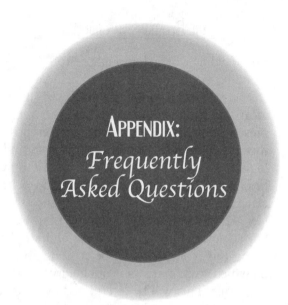

APPENDIX:
Frequently Asked Questions

Question: *I work for a private company with 100 employees. The owner, who is over 65, is in the hospital with a serious illness. There is a rumor that the company will be sold and that we will be laid off. How do I continue to do my work in such a miserable atmosphere?*

Answer: **The possibility of serious change creates new opportunities.** If you start to feel anxious, at home or at work, go to a private place and put the palm of your hand on your heart and breathe deeply. This exercise will help you stay grounded and support your ability to have an open heart and mind. This is an excellent exercise whenever you feel uprooted by fear, loss, or the negativity of others. When you are calm, use the four-step Harmonic Matching Process to attract your desired outcome. First, set your intention to align with a strong sense of well-being and to feel good regardless of what is happening around you. This will help you get rid of your worried thoughts. You will be commanding your subconscious to help you feel good. In the next step, you create your wish list for your ideal job. Don't limit yourself to working at your present company; be open to greater possibilities that are in alignment with your wishes and in the highest good of all (this includes your family members and others). With step three, you believe you can have what you desire. Create a staircase diagram (see Figure 7-1) to map out your vision by developing achievable goals, objectives, and strategies. In doing this work, you will be creating a foundation on which you can trust in your ability to attract what you want. This will be interpreted by your subconscious as a command to attract the ideal work situation. Finally, when you release the outcome, you let go, knowing that when we hold on too tight that means we are afraid. Fear always gets in the way of attracting an ideal situation. When we are fearful, we tend to settle for something less than we desire. We can also become immobilized by fear and unable to take inspired action that will help us create a positive outcome. Set intentions to feel peaceful and happy regardless of what is happening around you. As you come into resonance with this higher consciousness, your staircase will turn into an elevator and doors will open for you.

Q: *The HR person fired my best friend at work and accused him of watching porn on his computer. I am so angry at the HR person that I can barely look at him. This anger is preventing me from getting my work done.*

A: **When we take on the anger of others, we serve no one,** least of all our family and friends. The sooner you can release your anger, the sooner you can help your friend get past what happened and create something positive from this situation. If I were in your shoes, I'd set the intention to be a great support to my friend and to help him move into something better. By doing this, you will be commanding your subconscious to align with feelings of peace and well-being. Until you align with well-being, you can easily fall prey to mis-creating. You may even spend hours venting about what happened and reinforcing victim consciousness in yourself or your friend. Help your friend by helping yourself first. Once you have released your anger, you can help inspire him to learn from what happened and create a different experience in the future that can lead to better opportunities for him.

Q: *My company has hired an inappropriate salesperson. She is loud. You can hear her from one end of the building to the other. I am thinking of quitting.*

A: **I have had similar experiences.** What I have discovered is that setting my intention for my work environment was very helpful. Once you do this, you will be inspired to handle this situation in the most effective manner. For instance, you might find that talking with the salesperson about her voice is highly effective. Oftentimes we assume that we can't approach a person about a concern, but if we set an intention that the conversation will go very well and that both of you will come to an ideal resolution, you are pre-paving the situation. Pre-paving is a technique we use to create the way we want something to turn out. After we pre-pave, we open ourselves to an outcome better than we might expect. It's a technique you can use to command your subconscious to inspire and guide your words, actions, and even your body language so that the action you take results in a positive outcome. While pre-paving the meeting with your coworker, you might consider thinking positive thoughts, such as, *She will be grateful that I took the initiative to say something to her*. Or, *She probably has no idea that her voice is heard throughout the building and she will be glad that I am letting her know this. She is a caring and responsible person and I expect that she will be very responsive to me bringing this to her attention.* By pre-paving and seeing your coworker as caring and considerate, you create the foundation for a very positive outcome.

Q: *The woman at the next desk is undergoing some type of depression. She is absent with some illness every other day, and I have had to pick up the slack. I am now working overtime. I am resentful. What can I do?*

A: **Set the intention to be a great team member who is highly productive.** Set another intention to attract a workload that is manageable. Once you have set these intentions, you will be inspired to handle this situation in the most effective manner. It is not wise to sit and stew about things you cannot control. This just pushes you down into a lower vibrational consciousness and sets you up to experience more of the same. Tolerating, as opposed to being proactive, will decrease your productivity and minimize your cooperative spirit. If you wait too long to speak up, then you're sabotaging yourself. Once you've set your intentions, try talking with your boss about the depressed woman. Perhaps she can be referred to an employee assistance program (EAP) to get help and support. Pre-pave the conversation the way you want it to go and then be open-minded to what your boss has to say. If you are venting to your family or friends, stop doing so. Stay completely focused on being proactive. Set the intention to have a conversation with your boss at a time that he or she can hear you without interruptions. Include in your intention the idea that you and your boss

will be open-minded and creative in finding an expedi-
tious and ideal solution to this situation.

Q: *My direct manager has an outside business and uses the office phone to make calls about her other business. She is making mistakes, and I am covering up for her.*

A: **I can understand that this places you in an awkward position,** because it's your boss who is misusing the company telephone. However, covering up for anyone means that you are out of integrity. When we are out of integrity, we lose self-respect, and self-respect is the foundation of our creative energies. I suggest that you discuss this issue with her, but before you do, make sure to pre-pave how you want the discussion to be received. Also consider setting the intention to work only with people of the highest degree of integrity along with other items on your wish list for your work environment. Then be prepared that a shift is coming. Either your boss will rise to a higher level of integrity or you will attract a situation that matches your desires. Set up a private meeting with your manager to explain how you feel and to inform her that you have been covering up for her. Let her know that you cannot continue covering up for her and ask her to manage her phone calls for her other business using her time and her dime. By pre-paving this discussion, you will be inspired to handle the situation in a way that is in everyone's highest good.

Q: *My husband is African-American and I am Japanese. We have conflicting ideas about how to handle our differences. He feels that he should speak up and make it known when he is angry. My culture believes that you handle things in a quiet way without raising your voice. He says this is unhealthy and that I will die of a heart attack if I don't "let it all out." I think he just wants to have a screaming match, and I'm not going to give it to him. How would you suggest that we deal with our differences in handling conflict?*

A: **Differences occur in all close relationships.** Sometimes these differences arise from cultural background, but they can also arise from personal preferences or other circumstances. Unresolved conflict leads to mistrust, assumptions about the other person, and a breakdown in the relationship. When we candidly talk about our differences, then our relationships can be transformed to a higher, more intimate level. It is important, therefore, to speak up, and openly and honestly talk about your opinions, perceptions, and feelings. This can be accomplished most effectively if we do it in a nonjudgmental way and in a calm, thoughtful manner. When we desire resolution, then we will speak to the other person in a respectful way so he or she can hear what we are saying. But when we raise our voices, yell, or scream, we put up barriers between ourselves and others that prohibit us from resolving our differences. Staying in control of our emotions during candid discussions is a valuable skill that can be developed. Ground rules for communication can help us stay centered when we are addressing emotionally charged issues. Develop guidelines and come to an agreement in using them to address differences in your relationship.

Q: *Two of our vice presidents are married to each other. One has stopped performing. He comes in late, takes long lunch hours, and is absent a lot. This couple is a favorite of the owner. Can anything be done?*

A: **I can certainly empathize with your frustration and concerns in this situation.** If I were in your position, I would ask myself, *How does the behavior of these individuals impact me and/or the clients we serve?* If it does not impact either you or the company's clients, then it's best to stay focused on doing your job and not involve yourself with the behavior of others. However, if someone's actions negatively impact you or the clients you serve, then it's time to discuss this directly with the vice presidents. Pre-pave your meeting to be harmonious and to be in the highest good of all concerned. Create an image in your mind of how you want the meeting to be experienced by you and them. By doing this, you are accessing the power of your subconscious to create your desires. Please be aware that pre-paving does not guarantee that you will get the results you want, as you cannot control the decisions of other people. You must release the outcome and know that when you pre-pave, you are doing your part to co-create the optimal situation. As you become more confident in your ability to be a deliberate creator by correlating your thoughts, beliefs, and emotions with what you are attracting, you will naturally be aligned with a consciousness of well-being. Aligning with well-being means that you trust that you can attract your desires—either this or something better—though it does not always occur the way we anticipate. Get your resume ready and open up to possibilities in and outside of your current employment.

Q: I manage a warehouse. One of our employees brings his baby python to work with him. Our HR person is mean, and I don't want to go to her. I also don't want to get into trouble if things get out of hand with the snake.

A: **You have to take a risk in one direction or another, or you will be living in fear,** which is not conducive to being productive, happy, or even content. In this case, I would highly recommend that you deal directly with the employee who is bringing the snake to work. Let the employee know that you would like him to leave the python at home. If he does not respect your wishes, then inform him that you will need to report the situation to the HR department.

Remember to set intentions to take risks that are in your highest good and the highest good of all concerned. Allow yourself to be inspired into action. In addition, you can pre-pave for the future by creating a wish list for how you want various areas of your life to be experienced. You can create a wish list for home and work. Then, follow the four-step Harmonic Matching Process to align your consciousness with your desires, which will inspire the actions you take.

Q: *I want a new neighbor. The woman next door is mean and nasty. I've tried talking with her, but she always closes her door in my face. I'd really like to give her a piece of my mind. How can I stay focused on what I want to create and at the same time release the outcome?*

A: **Staying focused on what you want to create** does not mean that you have to think about it all the time. It means that your thoughts are in harmony with your desires. If your peace of mind or happiness is on hold, waiting for your neighbor to change her behavior or move away, then you will be waiting a long time. Even if she does leave, you will attract someone just like her...or even less pleasant. You can release the outcome by trusting in your ability to create your desires and knowing that if you have set the intention for your highest good, it will be forthcoming. It is through our personal experiences that we learn to trust in ourselves and in the process of co-creation. Begin by noticing your thoughts, beliefs, and feelings, and correlating them with what you are attracting. As you do this, you will learn more about yourself and what you are holding in your consciousness that is causing you to attract your experiences. In time, you will see the validity of the Harmonic Matching Process of co-creation.

Q: *Every time someone gets married or has a baby, we have an office collection. Because people are always coming and going, I have contributed greatly to people's presents. I'm tired of doing this. How do I talk about this in the office without seeming selfish?*

A: **If it doesn't feel good to do it, then don't do it.** However, I would ask myself a significant question: *How would I feel if I were terminating my employment, and my co-workers neither had a farewell celebration for me nor gave me a gift?* I would also ask this question: *How would I feel if someone terminated her employment and I did not go out of my way to let her know I appreciated her?* Appreciation does not, of course, have to come in the form of a tangible gift. It is very powerful to give someone a letter stating what you appreciated about her and citing the positive impact she had on you. Perhaps you could start a new tradition. I recommend that you discuss these ideas with others in your office, not from a perspective of complaining about spending the money but from a perspective of how best to celebrate the employee who is leaving. Most individuals want to feel appreciated, and a tangible gift does not necessarily provide this. Oftentimes, a gift from the heart—such as a letter of appreciation—is the most meaningful gift someone can give another.

Q: *I'm hoping to be promoted to a senior vice president position, but the division under me works slowly and is not as productive as I would like them to be. How do I get them to work harder and faster so I will look good to my boss?*

A: **The stronger and more positive your dominant vibration is about a particular desire,** the more quickly you will become a harmonic match to it. Be aware that you are focused on the negative. You're judging and impatient about the people who report to you, and so you are not in a position to inspire them to be more productive. I suggest setting your intention to align your thoughts with what you desire rather than what you fear. In this way, you will be commanding your subconscious to inspire you to take appropriate action to enhance the performance of your team members.

Q: *How is Harmonic Matching different from positive thinking? I have been saying affirmations for a year about attracting new friends. I'm still waiting for them to appear.*

A: **Harmonic Matching takes the concept of positive thinking to a feeling level.** Each of us has a vibrational consciousness that is determined by our thoughts, beliefs, and emotions. In general, our consciousness is aligned with either our desire or the fear of not having what we want. When we are aligned with our desires, we trust in our ability to create and feel a sense of well-being. When we are aligned with our fears, we tend to focus on not having enough of whatever we want. To attract and create what you want, you must first align with the feeling or essence of your desire. For instance, do you want new friends for companionship, to date, to participate in a particular activity with? Do you want someone to party with, go skiing with, or work on a project with? Once you discover the essence of your desire, you must find ways to align with this essence. Because Harmonic Matching is about creating a resonance with your desire, it is imperative that you create the feeling first. With the feeling in place, you naturally attract and create what you want with ease. If you *feel* lonely, you cannot attract friends, regardless of how many affirmations you say. You will only attract more reasons to feel lonely. Instead, create the essence of what you think more friendships will offer you through visual imagery, and in time, and probably when you least expect it, you will create resonance with your desire.

Q: *I am sick and tired of working with lazy people. I would like to work with people who are go-getters and take pride in the outcomes of our projects. How can I turn what I am currently attracting into something desirable using Harmonic Matching techniques?*

A: **To attract something different,** you must become a harmonic match to what you desire rather than what you dislike. Otherwise, you will continually attract what you resist. In this situation, write on your wish list that you want to work with people who are responsible, who have integrity, and who want to do a good job. Don't write what you don't want. Next, let's take it beyond positive thinking and actually raise your vibrational consciousness by shifting your feelings from judgment to focusing on your desires. For example, you might shift your feelings by saying, *Everyone has a right to their own value system. Perhaps the people I work with feel that they are doing a good job. Some of them may be doing the best that they know how to do. After all, we weren't really trained or given instructions about how to proceed with this project. I have a lot more experience than many of my coworkers; some of them are just out of college and this is their first job. Maybe I need to be a little more generous when I look at them.* **Your goal here is to access thoughts that are believable** and that bring you to a higher vibrational consciousness. As long as you judge people or situations, anything or anyone, you will continue to attract what you are giving attention to. When you release judgment, however, you can begin to resonate with your desires. Creating a more positive "feeling tone" about your coworkers on this issue will help you to shift your consciousness. Once you've succeeded in creating the feeling tone, you will be a harmonic match for your desire rather than what you are resisting.

Q: *I created a wish list for attracting an intimate relationship and included "for my highest good and the highest good for all concerned." Then I met a really nice man at work whom I like very much, but there are a several qualities he lacks that I would prefer in a long-term companion. In addition, it's a sticky situation, dating someone at work. Should I forget about trying to attract someone else and assume this man is in my best interests?*

A: **Although it may be in your best interests to be with this individual,** that does not necessarily translate into his being your ideal long-term partner or spouse. Sometimes we attract individuals into our experience who prepare us for what we really desire. These individuals are still in our highest good, even though we may not be in a relationship with them forever. Consider revising your wish list to incorporate your new, true preferences. If this man you have recently met is a harmonic match for your desires, then it will become obvious in time. Let your feelings be your guiding light.

Q: *Why is it that my friends keep leaving me? I even have trouble keeping a boyfriend.*

A: **When people leave relationships, they are saying yes to something else in their lives.** Their leaving does not mean that you are doing something wrong. It may simply indicate that you are fearful of loss, and because of this you keep attracting situations that re-create a feeling of loss for you. It may be helpful for you to seek more knowledge about the reasons individuals leave the relationship. You may want to ask a few of your friends if there was anything that happened between you and them that needed to be resolved. In this way you are opening yourself to learning from the experience. Knowledge of others' perceptions of us is powerful.

Let me also bring this to your attention: your question implies that you feel rejected and that you are questioning your self-worth. Remember that it may not be about you. Let the people in your life make their own choices without judging them or yourself. To raise your vibrational consciousness, you will want to stop focusing your attention on friends leaving and visualize them staying. As you begin to believe in the possibility of receiving your desires, your dominant vibration will shift to support you in creating all you want.

Q: *My fiancé and I get along fantastically, but his daughter is a spoiled brat. I do not get along with her—there is a lot of tension between us. I'm afraid he will call off the wedding if something doesn't change. He says we drive him nuts.*

A: **First of all, be aware of your emotions.** When you feel tension or fear about something you are not coming from a place of well-being, thus you cannot be a harmonic match for your desires. Shift your focus to the quality of your relationship with your partner rather than trying to control your partner to stay in the relationship. Set intentions to create a harmonious relationship with the daughter, one that is in the highest good for all concerned. Try visualizing an ideal situation with your fiancé and his daughter and then create a wish list that stems from your vision of the optimal family life. Allow yourself to be inspired to create something different than what the past might dictate. Stay open and allow yourself to be guided by your intuition. Let your actions be inspired.

Q: *My coworker and I both made our wish lists for a new job. We put good thoughts around our desires. She attracted a great opportunity in less than two weeks—and I'm still waiting for an interview. Why? What went wrong?*

A: **As long as you are in a *waiting* mode, you will con-tinue to be at a standstill.** Shift your focus from waiting for, longing for, and wanting something or someone to make you happy, peaceful, secure, or abundant, to feeling good about what you are doing in your current job. As you let go of trying so hard and appreciate where you are now, you will attract your desires.

Q: *I don't like my current supervisor. I really want to report to one particular person at work. I respect how she operates, and she has a lot of integrity. She is a good role model and mentor to me. How can I get reassigned to this woman I respect?*

A: **It is important to follow the four-step Harmonic Matching Process.** In your situation, you need to focus on step four, Release the Outcome. When we focus on bringing a specific person into our experience, we place our peace of mind and happiness on hold as we wait for the relationship to come to fruition. This keeps our de-sires just beyond our reach because, vibrationally, we are aligned with the mindset of scarcity. We think, *There is only one person who can meet my intentions.* Scarcity con-sciousness is out of alignment with attracting our desires. Stay focused on your preferences and on the qualities of the person you want to report to rather than on a par-ticular individual. Remember to set the intention for the highest good for all concerned. Relax and set your in-tention to align with wholeness and well-being. As you harmonize with the essence of well-being, you will attract your optimal supervisor.

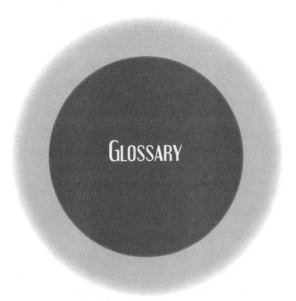

GLOSSARY

Aligned action: An action that is a harmonic (vibrational) match with the end result. All actions are aligned with the thoughts, emotions, and beliefs (vibrations) that created them. When we consciously align our actions, we are deliberately setting an intention to attract our desires by shifting our thoughts, beliefs, and emotions to be in harmony with what we want to attract or create.

Allowing: Freedom from the negative feelings that judgmental thoughts create. Allowing is different from tolerating, which implies looking down from a position of superiority and putting up with something or someone causing negative emotions about the situation or person. Because allowing is not resisting the way life is, it creates a positive emotional state. Allowing involves accepting the fact that everyone has undesirable experiences. It means choosing to learn from experiences rather than judging, worrying, or putting other negative thoughts around ourselves or others. Allowing involves feeling love and compassion for ourselves and for all others.

Co-creating: When two or more people come together to reach a goal, find a solution, create something new, or form a new bond. Co-creating is allowing the thoughts, beliefs, and emotions (vibrations) of others to influence what we create. Co-creating can have desirable or undesirable outcomes, depending upon the intentions and processes used by the people involved. Teamwork is an example of co-creating.

Deliberate creation: The process of aligning thoughts, beliefs, and emotions with our desire.

Desire: A strong wish, something for which we long or hope.

Dominant intention: The intention that overrides all other intentions when intentions contradict one another.

Dominant vibration: It magnetizes our experiences and is determined by the combined frequency of our thoughts, beliefs, and feelings regarding a particular desire. (*See also* Prevailing vibration.)

Emotions: Feelings that create a vibration that moves our thoughts and desires through space and time. The stronger the emotion, the more powerful the movement, which can be in the direction of our desires or in the direction of our fears. Emotions demonstrate whether our thoughts are focused on desires or whether they are focused on our fears of not having what we want.

Energize: To attract someone or something through our vibrational consciousness. When we energize something, we are projecting thoughts that are in alignment or harmony with our vibration, whether it is desired or undesired.

Feeling tone: The level of intensity of the emotion associated with a particular desire. Can be positive or negative.

Frequency: The rate of movement of energy in wave formations.

Harmonic Matching: The deliberate intention to attract our desires. (The same as vibrational matching.)

Harmonic Matching Process: The four-step process that aligns thoughts, beliefs, and emotions. The steps are (1) creating feel-good moments, (2) identifying desires, (3) activating intentions, and (4) releasing the outcome.

Harmonic vibration: The combined thoughts, emotions, and beliefs that we project toward something we desire or do not desire.

Highest degree of integrity: Integrity means being personally integrated or whole, finding the common ground of our core beliefs, and bringing it into all parts of our lives. Living from the highest degree of integrity means applying the guiding principle, which is asking ourselves what feels right and true to our heart in each situation. There is no right or wrong answer or logical set of rules to follow that can be applied to every circumstance.

Highest good: The best outcome for all. Allowing the pure vibration of consciousness to inspire and guide us so we can transcend perceived limitations and create desirable synchronistic events.

Integrity: Truthfulness with regard to actions that are consistent with the values we hold in our consciousness.

Intention: Blending strong desire with strong belief to create a deliberate outcome.

Intuition: From the Latin word *intueri*, which means "to look within," "to contemplate," or "to regard inwardly." When we pay attention to our feelings, we can strengthen our intuitive abilities. Intuition is the higher inner guidance that is part of our consciousness.

Law of Attraction: Vibrations of similar frequencies that are magnetized to each other. In essence, thought draws in other thoughts of a similar vibration.

Living outside of integrity: Compromising our values, beliefs, and/or principles. This violates our inner sense of wholeness. As the cliché says, we are living a lie.

Magnetic attraction: The dominant vibrational frequencies of two individuals in resonance. The stronger the resonance between two people, the stronger the attraction is. All of life is an interaction with the vibrational consciousness of others, which means we attract what we project into the world as well as what we focus on.

Negative emotion: Indicator that our thoughts are focused on the fear of *not* having what we want.

Optimism: Considering the glass to be half full, not half empty (which is pessimism). Optimism is the natural orientation when you believe that the world is abundant with all you need to fulfill your wishes. When we are optimistic, we minimize the impact of undesirable events and focus our attention on what we can learn from the experience.

Optimistic viewpoint: Getting the most value from every experience and anticipating positive outcomes in the future. Valuing every experience as one from which positive changes can be derived to ensure more desirable results.

Pessimism: Perception that the glass is half empty. Having a negative view of life and blaming ourselves or others when outcomes are undesirable.

Positive emotion: Indicator that we are giving attention to what we desire. Our thoughts are focused on what we want rather than what we fear.

Positive self-esteem: Belief that we are a valuable human being who is worthy of receiving unconditional love and capable of giving the same.

Pre-paving: A technique used to harmonize our vibration with the intent of attracting and creating desirable outcomes. Pre-paving involves aligning thoughts, beliefs, and emotions in the direction of our desires or intentions.

Prevailing vibration: Magnetizes our experiences. It is determined by the combined frequency of our thoughts, beliefs, and feelings regarding a particular desire. (Same as dominant vibration.)

Resonance: Two frequencies attuned to each other, vibrations moving together in the same wave pattern. Resonance is the fundamental principle of the Law of Attraction ("like attracts like"), which is universal. In music, when we strike the middle C of a piano, the other nine Cs on the keyboard begin to vibrate with it, even though they are untouched. Although other keys also absorb the energy of the touched middle C, only those with the same frequency sound.

Resonance at a high vibration: Having or expressing a sense of harmony with someone or something that creates a positive emotion in us.

Resonance at a low vibration: A connection with another person that creates stress and pain. Not feeling good about ourselves, having other negative emotions.

Scarcity consciousness: A belief that that we lack something that we need or want; feeling that we do not have enough of whatever we desire. Putting our peace of mind or happiness on hold waiting for something or someone to come into our lives because we believe we need that person or thing to feel whole.

Self-love: Filling up with love from within. We can enhance our self-love by cultivating an optimistic attitude and being compassionate and nonjudgmental about ourselves.

Subconscious: Whereas the conscious mind includes what we are aware of, the subconscious operates outside our awareness, or, as it is believed, "deep inside" us. Our subconscious supports us in affirming our beliefs about ourselves, others, situations, and circumstances.

Superego: In Sigmund Freud's model of the psyche, the critical, moralizing voice, that of the "parent" judging or criticizing the "child." The source of moralistic judgments toward ourselves and others.

Synchronicity and synchronistic resonance: Jung's version of coincidence that is not quite coincidental—when the right people, things, or events show up at the right time, when frequencies align at the same time and in a meaningful way, something other than the probability of chance is involved.

Vibration: Movement of energy in wave formations. Integration of our thoughts, beliefs, and emotions that make up our consciousness.

Vibrational consciousness: The awareness of the state of our thoughts, emotions, and beliefs, which can be positive or negative, higher or lower. When we are focused in the direction of our desires and aligned with well-being, our vibrational consciousness level is high and we attract good things we desire. When we are focused on our fears, our vibrational consciousness level is low and we attract one-sided, aggressive communication and engage in right/wrong or black/white thinking. As we raise our vibration, we come into harmony with others and attract those who, like us, operate from integrity and take responsibility for themselves.

Vibrational matching: The deliberate intention to attract our desires by aligning and focusing our thoughts, emotions, and beliefs with what we want.

Vibrational synchronicity: Alignment of frequencies in such a way that a meaningful coincidence of two or more events occurs. Something other than the probability of chance is involved.

Want: A desire, a strong wish, something we long or hope for.

Wanting: The state of longing for something. When we are in a state of wanting, our peace of mind or happiness are on hold as we wait for a desire to come to fruition.

BIBLIOGRAPHY

American Psychological Association. Bethune, S., and J. Panlenar. *Media Information*. (Review of the APA press release "Stress a Major Health Problem in U.S., Warns APA.") Retrieved May 31, 2008, from American Psychological Association Website: *www.apa.org//.html*.

Aschenbach, Michael. *VISION 3000: The Transformation of Humanity in the New Millennium*. Coatesville, Penn.: Emerging Vision Media, 2006. (The concepts presented here are based on the writings of A.H. Almaas, which integrate the work of many other developmental psychologists, such as Margaret Mahler, D.W. Winnicott, Heinz Kohut, R.D. Laing, and others.)

Baumann, T. Lee, M.D. *God at the Speed of Light: The Melding of Science and Spirituality*, Virginia Beach, Va.: A.R.E. Press, 2002.

Billick, Brian, and Michael MacCambridge. *Competitive Leadership: Twelve Principles for Success*. Chicago, Ill.: Triumph Books, 2001.

Blanchard, Ken, and Norman Vincent Peale. *The Power of Ethical Management*. New York: William Morrow, 1988.

Bloomfield, Harold H., MD, Melba Colgrove, PhD and Peter McWilliams. *How to Survive the Loss of a Love*. Algonac, Mich.: Mary Books/Prelude Press, 1976, 1991, 2000.

Capra, Fritjof. *The Hidden Connections: Integrating the Biological, Cognitive, and Social Dimensions of Life into a Science of Sustainability*. New York: Doubleday, 2002.

Carnegie, Dale. *How to Win Friends and Influence People, Revised Edition*. New York: Pocket Books, 1982.

Davis, Laura. *The Courage to Heal Workbook*. New York: HarperCollins, 1990.

de Maat, Martin. "A Conversation With Martin de Maat." Interview in *The Monthly Aspectarian*, 1998.

Dyer, Wayne, W., PhD. *The Power of Intention*. Carlsbad, Calif.: Hay House, 2004.

Fisher, Linda R., and Rose L.Kennedy. *Traveling Through White Water: A Manager's Guide for Organizational Change*. Highland Park, Ill.: K/F Publications, 1989.

Gallup Management Journal. Retrieved May 31, 2008 from the Gallup Organization Website: *http://gmj.gallup. com///Friends-Book-Center.aspx*.

Gelsz, Mary B. "Research Plan Developed to Study the Relationship Between Social Connectedness and Health." Robert Wood Johnson Foundation, December 2003.

Gerber, Richard, MD. *Vibrational Medicine*. Rochester, Vt.: Bear and Company, 2001.

Hawkins, David R., MD, PhD. *Power vs. Force: The Hidden Determinants of Human Behavior.* Carlsbad, Calif.: Hay House, 2002.

Hill, Napoleon. *Think and Grow Rich*. New York: Ballantine Books, 1960.

———. *The Amazing Power of Deliberate Intention: Living the Art of the Allowing.* Carlsbad, Calif.: Hay House, 2006.

Hicks, Esther, and Jerry Hicks. *Ask and it Is Given: Learning to Manifest Your Desires.* Carlsbad, Calif.: Hay House, 2004.

Jung, C.G. *Aion: Research into the Phenomenology of the Self.* Princeton, N.J.: Princeton University Press, 1969.

———. *The Archetypes and the Collective Unconscious.* Princeton, N.J.: Princeton University Press, 1959.

———. *Modern Man in Search of a Soul.* London: Kegan Paul, Trench, Trubler & Co., 1933.

———. *Synchronicity: An Acausal Connecting Principle.* Princeton, N.J.: Princeton University Press, 1969.

LeBoeuf, Michael, PhD. *The Greatest Management Principle in the World.* New York: G.P. Putnam's Sons, 1985.

Marriage and Families study. "Nuances of Interpersonal Relationships Influence Our Health, New Study Shows." Spring 2004.

McTaggart, Lynne. *The Field: The Quest for the Secret Force of the Universe.* New York: Harper Collins, 2002.

Murray, Bob, PhD, and M.S. Fortinberry. *Creating Optimism: A Proven, Seven-Step Program for Overcoming Depression,* New York: McGraw-Hill, 2004.

Newport, F. "The Challenges Women Face in Their Daily Lives." Message posted to Gallup News Service, April 14, 2000. Archived at *www.gallup.com///Women-Face-their-Daily-Lives.aspx.*

Radin, Dean, PhD. *The Conscious Universe.* New York: HarperEdge, 1997.

Rath, Tom, and Donald Clifton, PhD. *How Full Is Your Bucket? Positive Strategies for Work and Life.* New York: Gallup Press, 2004.

Robbins, Anthony. *Unlimited Power*. New York: Fawcett Columbine, published by Ballantine Books, a division of Random House, Inc., 1986.

Schroeder, Gerald L. *The Hidden Face of God: Science Reveals the Ultimate Truth*. New York: Pocket Books, 2001.

Seligman, Martin, EP, PhD. *Learned Optimism: How to Change Your Mind and Your Life*. New York: Pocket Books, 1991.

Shamdasani, Sonu. *Jung and the Making of Modern Psychology: The Dream of a Science*. Cambridge, UK: Cambridge University Press, 2003.

Targ, Russell. *Limitless Mind*. Novato, Calif.: New World Library, 2004.

Tiller, William A., PhD. *Science and Human Transformation: Subtle Energies, Intentionality and Consciousness*. Walnut Creek, Calif.: Pavior, 1997.

Willenz, Pam. *EurekAlert*. "Quality of relationships can affect health, indicated b level of stress hormones, according to new study." American Psychological Association, August 2000.

World Health Organization Constitution. July 22, 1946. Retrieved May 31, 2008 from the WHO Website: *www.who.int////.html*.

What Will You Do?

Consciousness does exist
throughout the Universe, in the mist,
to help you create your relationship bliss.

This one time and place...

Will you open your heart,
and align with grace?
To be with others,
and co-create?

Moments come and moments go...

What will you do,
to release the hate?
Tear down the walls,
and force open the gate?

What will you do
to bring in the new?

Will you look in the mirror and say,
I will be honest and true,
each and every day?

Or will you choose to disobey,
close the door and walk away?

It's time to open your heart,
time to expand your mind.
It's time to let down your guard,
time for you to align.

Moments come and moments go...

Which path might you take?
What way will you go?
Will you say yes,
or will you say no?

It is up to you
to allow relationship dreams to come true.
My dear, dear friend,
What will you do?

—Margaret McCraw
May 23, 2010

INDEX

activate your intentions, 184

affirmations and desires, 164

agreements, personal, 159

agreements, professional, 159

allowing, 196-197

ambiguous losses, 95-96

American Psychological Foundation, 21

assess your current state, 63-66

attraction, the law of, 123-124

barriers and resistance,186-191

beliefs, elevate your, 166-172

Billick, Brian, 11-13, 163

Bloomfield, Harold, 89

body language, 81-82

boosters, transformation, 180-184

boss relationship wish list, 148-149

Buck, Pearl S., 69

Carnegie, Dale, 29

Choices, 16

circumstances, surrender, 201-202

co-create with others from strength and equality, 208-209

co-create with others, 69-88

Colgrove, Melba, 89

communicating relationship goals to others, 155-161

249

communication do's, 71-75

communication, how your vibrational level affects, 75-81

Competitive Leadership, 13

conscious and subconscious motivators, 49-54

conscious motivators in relationships, 49-54

consciousness of abundance and success, fostering, 209-211

consciousness, scarcity, 37-41

creating versus mis-creating your desires, 150-152

creating wish lists, tips for, 146-147

day-to-day living after loss, coping with, 103

desires, creating versus mis-creating, 150-152

desires, identifying relationship, 152-154

dominant intention and vibration, 191-193

elevate your beliefs, 166-172

Emerson, Ralph Waldo, 97

emotional transformation, 124-129

empowering others, 6 ways, 67

enhancers and inhibitors of well-being, 128-129

enhancers, 15 relationship, 59-63

exercises, co-creating, 70-71

exercises, self-understanding, 66-67

expectations, clarity of, 137

fear, heart knows no, 15

fear, releasing, 186

feelings of inadequacy, release, 188

feelings, take responsibility for your, 72

forgiveness, 105-106

giving, lovingly versus sacrificial, 58-59

goals to others, communicating relationship, 155-161

gratitude, 197-199

growth after loss, 103-105

growth, 83

Harmonic Matching Process, 12

Harmonic Matching Process, 23, 29-45

Harmonic Matching, 30-41

healing from loss, 99-103

healing, 112

holding on and success, 186

identify your desires, 145-162

identifying relationship desires, 152-154

identity, moving to a new, 207-208

inhibitors and enhancers of well-being, 128-129

inhibitors, overcoming, 167-170

integrity and wholeness, 199-200

intentions, activate your, 184

intentions, plan, alignment, 179-180

intuition and self-love, 47-48

judgment, releasing, 187-188

leader's team relationship wish list, 149-150

letting go of resistance, 185-220

life's work, discover your, 176-179

light guidance system, traffic, 134-136

loses, 89-105

Loving Yourself, 31-34

Magnetic Attraction, 30

McWilliams, Peters, 89

memories,
focus on good, 119-121
creating feel-good, 119-144

motivators, conscious and subconscious, 49-54

Murray, Bob, 136

one-minute plan, 132

one-up/one-down style, 80

optimism, 201
cultivate, 136-137

outcome, release the, 185-220

outcomes, positive, 195-201

Pain, love knows no, 15

personal agreements, 159

positive relationships, toolbox for building, 59-63

professional agreements, 156

prophecy, self-fulfilling, 52-54

Ravens, Baltimore, 11

Reality and your focus, 34-37

recovery, stages of, 97-105

reframe undesirable situations, 206-208

relationship boundaries, 202-204

relationship desires, identifying, 152-154

relationship, recovering from the loss of a, 89-115

relationships and how we inhibit them, 56-57

relationships as matters of the heart, 17

relationships,
conscious motivators in, 49-54

subconscious factors in, 51

why we attract undesirable, 55

release the outcome, 185-220

resonance, 41

Robbins, Anthony, 145

Robert Wood Johnson Foundation, 21

self-love, 48

self-love/self-esteem, 200-201

self-talk, align your, 164-166

self-understanding, 47-67, 66-67

situations, reframe undesirable, 206-208

six ways to empower others, 67

sixty-minute plan, 133

stages of recovery, 97-105

staircase, build your, 173-176

state, asses your current, 63-66

style,
   aggressive, 78
   enhancing your, 139-141

success, holding on inhibits, 186

surviving, 111

thirty-minute plan, 132

thriving, 114

toolbox, 59-63, 107-110

transformation boosters, 180-184

transformation, emotional, 124-129

transformational boosters, 141-142, 161

transitions, processing organizational, 106-107

treatment, the silent, 79

trust and belief, 195

undesirable outcomes, learning from, 165

undesirable relationships, why we attract, 55

vibration, synchronicity and our prevailing, 43-45

vibrational style, high-level harmonic, 82-88

well-being,
   how to create, 131-133
   ten essentials to, 129-131

wish lists, 146-150
   boss relationship, 148-149
   tips for creating, 146-147

work, discover your life's, 176-179

World Mental health Organization, 22

yourself, feel good about, 121-123

Yourself, Loving, 31-34

ABOUT THE AUTHOR

MARGARET MCCRAW, PhD, MBA, LCSW-C, is a nationally recognized educator, keynote speaker, and trainer with more than 25 years of experience in organizational management and relationship issues. Founder and president of Behavioral Healthcare Consulting and Leadership Dynamics Group, Dr. McCraw provides executive coaching and training, and management consulting for businesses, nonprofits, and governmental agencies. She specializes in helping organizations create their vision through strategic planning and by changing the culture. In aligning with her belief that good relationships sustain good health, she has recently launched an accredited Board Certified Life Coach Training Program that attracts students from all over the world. In addition, students can expand their studies and earn a certificate as a Holistic Health Practitioner. She is also working on her next book, a study of the four-step Harmonic Matching Process in love relationships.

She uses the Harmonic Matching Process in consulting, coaching, and leadership training, and in her keynote speaking engagements. She resides in Baltimore, Maryland.

ABOUT DR. McCRAW'S ACCREDITED COACH TRAINING AND HOLISTIC HEALTH PRACTITIONER CERTIFICATION PROGRAM

Dr. McCraw offers an accredited fast-track training program for those who qualify to become a Master Life Coach and Holistic Health Practitioner using the four-step Harmonic Matching Process. Her training is very different from traditional life coach programs in several ways. The unique Harmonic Matching Process:

- Is based on sound psychological principles aligned with cognitive behavioral techniques.

- Offers continuing education credits for some healthcare professionals.

- Views clients as capable of holding themselves accountable, whereas many traditional coach training programs view the role of the coach as holding the client accountable.

- Is holistic in nature, which means that the coach is trained to address issues in all aspects of clients' lives, including relationships, health, career, prosperity consciousness, and integration of life mission and vision.

- Teaches coaches to guide clients to learn the processes and techniques to deliberately create desirable outcomes.

If you are someone who likes to help people, and if you are good at helping others solve difficult problems, then life coaching may be a profession you want to consider. You can learn more about Dr. McCraw's training by going to *www.margaretmccraw.com*.

~~~

She also offers the following consulting services to organizations and individuals:

- ✗ Keynote speaking.
- ✗ Executive coaching.
- ✗ Performance quality improvement.
- ✗ Strategic planning.
- ✗ Team building.
- ✗ Transition planning.
- ✗ Culture assessment.
- ✗ Leadership training.
- ✗ Customer service effectiveness.
- ✗ Business process re-engineering.
- ✗ Business plan development.
- ✗ Meeting facilitation.

Go to *www.margaretmccraw.com* for further information.